Homosexuality

Other Books of Related Interest:

Opposing Viewpoints Series

AIDS

Religion and Sexuality

At Issue Series

Sexually Transmitted Diseases

Current Controversies Series

Homosexuality

"Congress shall make no law . . . abridging the freedom of speech, or of the press."

First Amendment to the U.S. Constitution

The basic foundation of our democracy is the First Amendment guarantee of freedom of expression. The Opposing Viewpoints Series is dedicated to the concept of this basic freedom and the idea that it is more important to practice it than to enshrine it.

Homosexuality

Cynthia A. Bily, Book Editor

Christine Nasso, *Publisher*
Elizabeth Des Chenes, *Managing Editor*

For more information, contact:
Greenhaven Press
27500 Drake Rd.
Farmington Hills, MI 48331-3535
Or you can visit our Internet site at gale.cengage.com

Articles in Greenhaven Press anthologies are often edited for length to meet page requirements. In addition, original titles of these works are changed to clearly present the main thesis and to explicitly indicate the author's opinion. Every effort is made to ensure that Greenhaven Press accurately reflects the original intent of the authors. Every effort has been made to trace the owners of copyrighted material.

LIBRARY OF CONGRESS CATALOGING-IN-PUBLICATION DATA

Homosexuality / Cynthia A. Bily, book editor.
p. cm. -- (Opposing viewpoints)
Includes bibliographical references and index.
ISBN-13: 978-0-7377-4214-5 (hardcover)
ISBN-13: 978-0-7377-4215-2 (pbk.)
1. Homosexuality. I. Bily, Cynthia A.
HQ76.25.H67375 2008
306.76'6--dc22

2008024132

Printed in the United States of America
1 2 3 4 5 6 7 12 11 10 09 08

Contents

Why Consider Opposing Viewpoints?

> *"The only way in which a human being can make some approach to knowing the whole of a subject is by hearing what can be said about it by persons of every variety of opinion and studying all modes in which it can be looked at by every character of mind. No wise man ever acquired his wisdom in any mode but this."*
>
> *John Stuart Mill*

In our media-intensive culture it is not difficult to find differing opinions. Thousands of newspapers and magazines and dozens of radio and television talk shows resound with differing points of view. The difficulty lies in deciding which opinion to agree with and which "experts" seem the most credible. The more inundated we become with differing opinions and claims, the more essential it is to hone critical reading and thinking skills to evaluate these ideas. Opposing Viewpoints books address this problem directly by presenting stimulating debates that can be used to enhance and teach these skills. The varied opinions contained in each book examine many different aspects of a single issue. While examining these conveniently edited opposing views, readers can develop critical thinking skills such as the ability to compare and contrast authors' credibility, facts, argumentation styles, use of persuasive techniques, and other stylistic tools. In short, the Opposing Viewpoints Series is an ideal way to attain the higher-level thinking and reading skills so essential in a culture of diverse and contradictory opinions.

In addition to providing a tool for critical thinking, Opposing Viewpoints books challenge readers to question their own strongly held opinions and assumptions. Most people form their opinions on the basis of upbringing, peer pressure, and personal, cultural, or professional bias. By reading carefully balanced opposing views, readers must directly confront new ideas as well as the opinions of those with whom they disagree. This is not to simplistically argue that everyone who reads opposing views will—or should—change his or her opinion. Instead, the series enhances readers' understanding of their own views by encouraging confrontation with opposing ideas. Careful examination of others' views can lead to the readers' understanding of the logical inconsistencies in their own opinions, perspective on why they hold an opinion, and the consideration of the possibility that their opinion requires further evaluation.

Evaluating Other Opinions

To ensure that this type of examination occurs, Opposing Viewpoints books present all types of opinions. Prominent spokespeople on different sides of each issue as well as well-known professionals from many disciplines challenge the reader. An additional goal of the series is to provide a forum for other, less known, or even unpopular viewpoints. The opinion of an ordinary person who has had to make the decision to cut off life support from a terminally ill relative, for example, may be just as valuable and provide just as much insight as a medical ethicist's professional opinion. The editors have two additional purposes in including these less known views. One, the editors encourage readers to respect others' opinions—even when not enhanced by professional credibility. It is only by reading or listening to and objectively evaluating others' ideas that one can determine whether they are worthy of consideration. Two, the inclusion of such viewpoints encourages the important critical thinking skill of objectively evaluating an author's credentials and bias. This evaluation will illuminate an author's reasons for taking a particular stance on an issue and will aid in readers' evaluation of the author's ideas.

It is our hope that these books will give readers a deeper understanding of the issues debated and an appreciation of the complexity of even seemingly simple issues when good and honest people disagree. This awareness is particularly important in a democratic society such as ours in which people enter into public debate to determine the common good. Those with whom one disagrees should not be regarded as enemies but rather as people whose views deserve careful examination and may shed light on one's own.

Thomas Jefferson once said that "difference of opinion leads to inquiry, and inquiry to truth." Jefferson, a broadly educated man, argued that "if a nation expects to be ignorant and free . . . it expects what never was and never will be." As individuals and as a nation, it is imperative that we consider the opinions of others and examine them with skill and discernment. The Opposing Viewpoints Series is intended to help readers achieve this goal.

David L. Bender and Bruno Leone,
Founders

Introduction

> *"Throughout the series, she has been diligent . . . in her commitment to the inclusion of characters of different races, cultures, classes and degrees of physical beauty. It would, in fact, have been a glaring omission had none of the inhabitants of her world been homosexual."*
>
> *—Rebecca Traister, Salon.com*

> *"It's very disappointing that the author would have to make one of the characters gay. It's not a good example for our children, who really like the books and the movies. I think it encourages [homosexuality]."*
>
> *—Roberta Combs, Christian Coalition of America*

In 1997, British author J.K. Rowling published *Harry Potter and the Philosopher's Stone*, the first in a series of seven young adult novels about Harry Potter, a young wizard who confronts and ultimately defeats the evil Lord Voldemort. The adventures of Harry, his friends Ron and Hermione, and his mentor Albus Dumbledore, became unimaginably popular; by April 2008, the books had been translated into more than 60 languages, and all together more than 375 million copies of the books had been sold. The books have been popular with parents and teachers as well as with children, but they have also drawn controversy. Many readers believe the Harry Potter stories teach moral lessons about friendship, loyalty, and equality, but others believe the books encourage a dangerous fascination with witchcraft. Even as the books became best sellers, some parents and religious leaders across the United States called for them to be banned from classrooms and libraries. The controversy deepened in October 2007, a few months after publication of the seventh book, *Harry Potter and the Deathly Hallows*, when Rowling gave a talk at New York City's Carnegie Hall. Answering a question from the audience about whether Dumbledore, the headmaster at Harry's school, had ever been in love, Rowling responded, "I always saw Dumbledore as gay."

The news of Dumbledore's "outing" led to a brief but strenuous debate. For some readers, Dumbledore's sexual identity was welcome news. A column posted on the gaygamer.net Web site, for example, carried the title "This Just In: Dumbledore's on Our Team, Baby!" Others, including writer Linda Harvey, felt betrayed, and worried that parents would "continue to desert clear biblical teaching and allow their kids to maintain hero-worship of an 'out' homosexual." Some gay activists also felt betrayed, saying that if Rowling truly wished to treat homosexuality as a normal part of human life she would have dealt with the subject more frankly in her series, rather than waiting until after all of the books had been published. And some readers argued that the sexual orientation of a fictional character was a non-issue. Author Devra Renner contended that children would be less concerned than adults were about Dumbledore's sexual identity. Contributing to a blog for mothers in the Washington, D.C., area, she wrote, "I think my kids would find it more captivating to discuss a character's magical power than a character being gay."

The debate over Albus Dumbledore is just one example of a kind of controversy that has become more and more common in the past two or three decades, as gay men and women have become more visible, and discussions of sexual orientation have become more public. Previously, most gay men and lesbians lived "in the closet"; that is, they kept their sexual orientation a secret from all but their closest friends, out of fear of public and legal condemnation. There were no gay-straight alliances in schools, there were no openly gay characters on television shows, and same-sex couples did not generally reveal the nature of their relationships. But in 1992, Bill Clinton ran for president of the United States, promising to allow gay men and women to serve openly in the military. In 1997, the actor Ellen DeGeneres "came out" as a lesbian on the *Oprah Winfrey Show*, and her own character on the situation comedy *Ellen* came out shortly after. In 2004, Massachusetts became the first state in the nation to legally recognize same-sex marriage. In 2006, students at more than four thousand schools participated in the annual Day of Silence to protest harassment and bullying of gay and lesbian students, and were countered by a smaller group of students opposing acceptance of homosexuality by participating in a Day of Truth. In twenty-first century America, homosexuality is no longer a secret.

As gay men and women have gained confidence and public support, they have worked to improve their status in public life, and have increasingly asked for—even demanded—the same rights, responsibilities, and protections as their "straight" peers. These public demands have led to open debates in the media, in churches and schools, around the dining room table, and in the halls of government. And just as one group of people works to bring the topic out in the open in an attempt to show homosexuality as within the range of natural human behavior, another works just as hard to silence the debate in an attempt to protect young people from being exposed to ideas too complex for their understanding. Men and women of goodwill have struggled to find clear and fair answers to several questions: What are the causes of homosexuality? Should gay men and women serve in the military? Should same-sex couples be allowed to marry? Should schools teach about homosexuality? The authors in this volume present a range of answers to these important questions.

What Are the Causes of Homosexuality?

Chapter Preface

Central to the debate over homosexuality through the past quarter-century has been this question: Is it a choice? Many people believe that acting on same-sex attractions is morally wrong, and they believe that being gay, or "living the homosexual lifestyle," is nothing more than a poor choice, like choosing to steal a car or to tell a lie. Others believe that being gay or lesbian is innate, something a person is born with, and that gay men and lesbians can no more choose to be attracted to others of the same sex than they can choose their height or their eye color. For all of these people, establishing a cause for same-sex attraction is an important step in answering a moral question.

This divide is reflected even in the ways people speak about homosexuality. Some people use the term "sexual preference" to describe whether one is attracted to members of the same sex or to the opposite sex. The underlying message of this term, others argue, is that sexual identity is a choice, a preference. Many people—including most scientists—favor the term "sexual orientation," a term that implies that sexual attraction is an integral part of a person's identity.

Scientists have discovered several intriguing differences between "straight" men and women and those who are gay and lesbian. Although the data are not conclusive, it appears that variations in the size of specific parts of the brain, in the ratios between certain finger lengths, and even in the direction of hair swirls might indicate one's sexual orientation. For some gay men and lesbians, this is promising news. If it can be proven that their orientation is part of their biology, they can feel more confident of their place in a society, they believe, that will have to accept them as they are. But some gay men and lesbians have concerns. If sexual orientation can be traced to genetic code, they wonder, will DNA tests be able to determine the sexual orientation of someone who would rather keep that information private? Will parents be able to determine the sexual orientation of their children before birth, and might some parents hesitate to continue a pregnancy if they knew their child would be gay? Might science find ways to manipulate genetic code to "correct" homosexuality?

Others have tried to determine whether trauma in the womb or during childhood might cause a change in sexual orientation. They believe that homosexuality is a mental illness that can be treated and cured with proper therapy. Alan P. Medinger writes that "homosexuality is an aberration, the orientation is a disorder, and the behavior is pathological," and argues that society is right to try to prevent gay men and lesbians from harming themselves—and perhaps others.

According to the American Academy of Pediatrics, "sexual orientation probably is not determined by any one factor but by a combination of genetic, hormonal, and environmental influences." This suggests several lines of inquiry for scientists. As they grapple with a complicated scientific question, political, social, and religious activists—including the authors in this chapter—are looking over their shoulders, hoping for evidence that will help them win a moral debate.

VIEWPOINT 1

> *"Identical twins, who share 100 percent of their genes, show a higher chance of both being gay compared with fraternal twins."*

Homosexuality Is Influenced by Genetics

Robert Mitchum

In the following viewpoint, journalist Robert Mitchum describes an ongoing study of gay men and their brothers, part of an effort by researchers to identify a genetic cause for homosexuality. Physical traits have been tied to sexual orientation, Mitchum reports, but most studies of gay men have involved too few individuals for the studies to yield statistically significant results. Scientists involved in the research hope to establish a definite link between genetics and sexual orientation, but the viewpoint concludes that this new knowledge may create as many questions as it does solutions. Mitchum is a staff reporter for the Chicago Tribune.

As you read, consider the following questions:

1. According to the viewpoint, how many sets of gay brothers do the scientists hope to examine?

Robert Mitchum, "Study of Gay Brothers May Find Clues About Sexuality," *Chicago Tribune*, August 12, 2007.

2. How are Chicago researchers obtaining DNA from test subjects, as reported in the viewpoint?
3. Why do some critics worry about finding a biological component to sexual orientation, according to the viewpoint?

In Gregg Mierow's family, there were six boys, brothers who grew into two groups as they reached maturity: Three are gay, and three are straight.

"It seems innate to me," Mierow, who works in advertising and as a yoga teacher in Chicago, said of his homosexuality. "It doesn't seem like there's any choice involved, and it seemed very clear even when we were very young."

Mierow stumbled upon a chance to help prove that hunch at the Northalsted Market Days Festival [in Chicago] four years ago [in 2003]. Spotting a banner reading, "Wanted! Gay Men with a Gay Brother," he stopped by the booth and volunteered for what he thought would be little more than a survey.

Instead, Mierow found himself part of the Molecular Genetic Study of Sexual Orientation—the most extensive study yet to search for a genetic basis for homosexuality—embarked upon by a team of Chicago researchers from local universities.

The scientists hope that by gathering DNA samples, from 1,000 sets of gay brothers like the Mierows, they will be able to find genetic linkages smaller studies failed to detect. They'll be recruiting brothers again at the Halsted Street Festival this weekend [in 2007].

A Controversial Question

The results may ignite controversy, the researchers acknowledge, both by providing ammunition in the raging cultural war over homosexuality and by raising fears about ethically questionable applications like genetic profiling and prenatal testing.

But, they argue, the research is essential to our biological understanding of sexual behavior.

"If there are genetic contributions to sexual orientation, they will not remain hidden forever—the march of genetic science can't be stopped," said Timothy F. Murphy, bioethicist adviser to the study. "It's not a question of whether we should or should not do this research, it's that we make sure we're prepared to protect people from insidious uses of this science."

Although the question of whether homosexuality is a choice remains a hot topic for pundits, scientists are largely in agreement that sexual orientation is at least partially determined by biology.

Studies that compare identical and fraternal twins for the frequency of a particular behavioral trait have consistently suggested there are both genetic and environmental causes of homosexuality. Identical twins, who share 100 percent of their genes, show a higher chance of both being gay compared with fraternal twins, who typically share the same family environment but only half their genetic code.

Researchers also have found physical traits that correlate with homosexuality, from the relative size of certain brain areas associated with sexual behavior to seemingly irrelevant characteristics like hair whorl direction and finger-length ratios.

The Search for a "Gay Gene"

Inspired by the accumulating circumstantial evidence of genetic factors, researchers in the early '90s began trying to narrow down the wide expanse of DNA to a few promising regions. By comparing the genetic codes of gay brothers, who also share 50 percent of their genes, a "linkage study" tries to detect areas that show up in both men at a frequency higher than chance, suggesting one or more genes in that region might be linked to sexual orientation.

In 1993, geneticist Dean Hamer announced his group had found such a region on the X chromosome, which males in-

Genetic Differences in the Brain

The square highlights the brain region containing a patch of tissue known as INAH-3. The size of the region has been linked to sexual orientation.

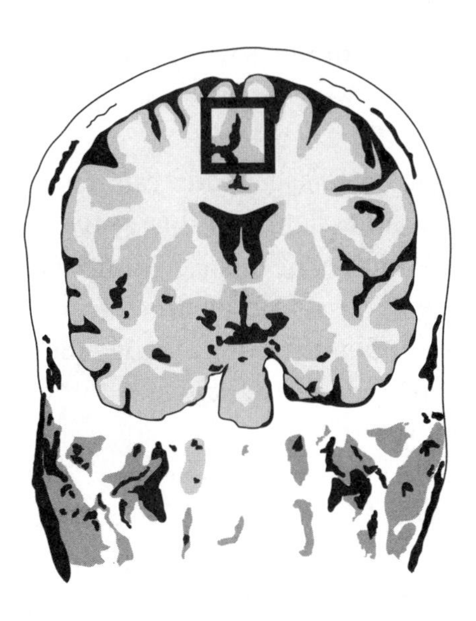

TAKEN FROM: Michael Abrams, "Born gay? Is homosexuality nature or nature? Science is homing in on the answer, " *Discover*, June 2007.

herit from their mothers. But the number of brother pairs used in the study was small, and subsequent studies failed to replicate Hamer's findings, throwing the result into question.

"In complex gene scenarios, people figured out that you need a larger sample size in order to get reasonable statistical power," said Dr. Alan Sanders, a psychiatrist at Evanston[, Illinois,] Northwestern Healthcare and the leader of the current study.

To increase the chances of finding genetic areas associated with homosexuality, Sanders proposed assembling almost ten times the sibling pairs of previous studies. The project received funding in 2001 and began recruiting subjects at gay pride festivals, through gay-oriented publications and on the Internet.

So far the Chicago researchers have obtained blood or saliva DNA samples and survey data from more than 600 brother sets, with several hundred other volunteers in the process of submitting one or the other. Sanders hopes to publish his findings from the first wave of DNA samples in a scientific journal sometime next year [in 2008].

Sanders cautioned a linkage study can single out only regions of the genetic code, not individual genes.

"One of the advantages of linkage studies is that we don't have to know those things ahead of time," Sanders said. "It's a big advantage here because we don't know about the biology of sexual orientation yet, so we can find the genes first and then study the biology."

Many Unanswered Questions

At this point, the researchers do not know what types of genes they may find; they could be related to hormones, sexual development or a completely unexpected system.

"The genes would probably be doing their work by affecting sexual differentiation of the brain during prenatal life," said J. Michael Bailey, a Northwestern University psychology professor involved with the project. "But what scientists are increasingly appreciating is that genes can affect a trait in ways you could never have guessed."

The hunt for specific genes that affect sexual orientation may take several years, but the implications of this eventual finding are being fiercely debated already.

"I think this kind of research receives a lot more criticism and attention because people often think it has profound implications for social and moral decisions," Bailey said. "This is a controversial area. Even though it fascinates people, it scares people from the research end."

Researchers involved with the project believe finding a genetic linkage will help settle arguments over whether homosexuality is a choice or an innate trait.

"A lot of times people we talk to see this research as providing evidence for something they may [have] already had a notion for, that sexual orientation is influenced by pretty early events out of their control," said Sanders.

Sanders also suggested that as proof of biological predisposition grows, so too does acceptance and tolerance of homosexuals. A Gallup poll conducted in May [2007] indicated 42 percent of the surveyed population believes homosexuality is biologically determined—the highest percentage witnessed in 30 years of polling.

Will Science Inspire Acceptance?

Study volunteer Jason Palmer of Chicago said he hopes evidence of a biological source for homosexuality would change people's opinions on sexual orientation.

"Our strongest opponents are the religious right, many of whom feel that God does not make mistakes," Palmer said. "So if it's a genetic factor and proven, perhaps many of them will find an acceptance for homosexuals."

But some outside observers worry about how proof of a genetic component to homosexuality might be used politically and even medically.

"If you do research on any human behaviors that would allow us either to treat the behavior or to prevent it altogether by prenatal testing, you have got to ask yourself serious questions about societal context in which this type of research takes place," said Udo Schuklenk, a professor of philosophy at Queen's University in Kingston, Ontario.

Critics fear identifying a biological component will lead to prenatal testing and perhaps even treatments for homosexuality. While both Sanders and Bailey expressed doubt about the scientific feasibility or public demand for such applications, Schuklenk suggested they were not considering the worldwide implications.

"I understand why U.S. gays want to know why gay people are gay and understand where they are coming from—there are legal reasons, and the agenda is progressive within the context of the United States," said Schuklenk. "What worries me is that they show a complete disregard of repercussions of research on the international scale, for gay people in societies where civil rights are not as well-protected."

Hopes for the Future

Mierow said he considered the potential negative ramifications when he volunteered for the study but trusted that changing social views on homosexuality will intervene.

"I hope that by the time science gets to the point [of prenatal testing], society would have progressed enough to not have those feelings," Mierow said. "I feel like I have more trust in science. It seems like a lot of the bigotry is coming out of religion."

"People who say that, 'We shouldn't know X because knowing X is dangerous,' to me those are the dangerous people," Bailey added. "They have provided no good evidence that knowing things is risky; ignorance is what messes us up."

For now, these discussions will remain largely theoretical until the results of Sanders' study, as well as others in progress around the country, begin to be released.

As Bailey noted, the results won't just add to knowledge about the roots of homosexuality, they may also answer more general questions about gender and sexuality.

"Knowing what causes sexual orientation is important scientifically," he said. "It's an important aspect of who we are and will provide knowledge about the development of gender, how men and women differ from each other."

VIEWPOINT 2

"The research suggests that early on in the womb . . . something fundamental to sexual orientation is happening."

Homosexuality Is Influenced by Prenatal Conditions

Neil Swidey

In the following viewpoint, journalist Neil Swidey considers the evidence that sexual orientation is caused by something that happens in the womb, before a child is born. After explaining the roles of the X and Y chromosomes and of various hormones in sexual development, he concludes that—in men, at least—sexual orientation appears to be established before birth.

Swidey is an award-winning member of the staff of the Boston Globe Magazine. *His article "What Makes People Gay?", from which this viewpoint was excerpted, was included in the anthology* The Best American Science Writing 2006.

As you read, consider the following questions:

1. According to the mother of the twins called Thomas and Patrick, how long have the two boys shown markedly different behaviors?

Neil Swidey, "What Makes People Gay?" www.boston.com., August 14, 2005. Republished with permission of *The Boston Globe*, conveyed through Copyright Clearance Center, Inc.

2. As explained in the viewpoint, what is the name of one of the brain structures that influences sexual behavior?
3. According to the author, what are some of the reasons that it is difficult to find conclusive evidence for the causes of sexual orientation?

With crystal-blue eyes, wavy hair, and freshly scrubbed faces, the boys look as though they stepped out of a Pottery Barn Kids catalog. They are 7-year-old twins. I'll call them Thomas and Patrick; their parents agreed to let me meet the boys as long as I didn't use their real names.

Spend five seconds with them, and there can be no doubt that they are identical twins—so identical even they can't tell each other apart in photographs. Spend five minutes with them, and their profound differences begin to emerge.

Patrick is social, thoughtful, attentive. He repeatedly addresses me by name. Thomas is physical, spontaneous, a bit distracted. Just minutes after meeting me outside a coffee shop, he punches me in the upper arm, yells, "Gray punch buggy!" and then points to a Volkswagen Beetle cruising past us. It's a hard punch. They horse around like typical brothers, but Patrick's punches are less forceful and his voice is higher. Thomas charges at his brother, arms flexed in front of him like a mini-bodybuilder. The differences are subtle—they're 7-year-old boys, after all—but they are there.

The Twins Exhibit Differences

When the twins were 2, Patrick found his mother's shoes. He liked wearing them. Thomas tried on his father's once but didn't see the point.

When they were 3, Thomas blurted out that toy guns were his favorite things. Patrick piped up that his were the Barbie dolls he discovered at day care.

When the twins were 5, Thomas announced he was going to be a monster for Halloween. Patrick said he was going to be a princess. Thomas said he couldn't do that, because other kids would laugh at him. Patrick seemed puzzled. "Then I'll be Batman," he said.

Their mother—intelligent, warm, and open-minded—found herself conflicted. She wanted Patrick—whose playmates have always been girls, never boys—to be himself, but she worried his feminine behavior would expose him to ridicule and pain. She decided to allow him free expression at home while setting some limits in public.

That worked until last year, when a school official called to say Patrick was making his classmates uncomfortable. He kept insisting that he was a girl.

Patrick exhibits behavior called childhood gender nonconformity, or CGN. This doesn't describe a boy who has a doll somewhere in his toy collection or tried on his sister's Snow White outfit once, but rather one who consistently exhibits a host of strongly feminine traits and interests while avoiding boy-typical behavior like rough-and-tumble play. There's been considerable research into this phenomenon, particularly in males, including a study that followed boys from an early age into early adulthood. The data suggest there is a very good chance Patrick will grow up to be homosexual. Not all homosexual men show this extremely feminine behavior as young boys. But the research indicates that, of the boys who do exhibit CGN, about 75 percent of them—perhaps more—turn out to be gay or bisexual.

Beyond Nature—Nurture

What makes the case of Patrick and Thomas so fascinating is that it calls into question both of the dominant theories in the long-running debate over what makes people gay: nature or nurture, genes or learned behavior. As identical twins, Patrick and Thomas began as genetic clones. From the moment they came out of their mother's womb, their environment was about as close to identical as possible—being fed, changed, and plopped into their car seats the same way, having similar relationships with the same nurturing father and mother. Yet before either boy could talk, one showed highly feminine traits while the other appeared to be "all boy," as the moms at the playgrounds say with apologetic shrugs.

"That my sons were different the second they were born, there is no question about it," says the twins' mother.

So what happened between their identical genetic starting point and their births? They spent nine months in utero. In the hunt for what causes people to be gay or straight, that's now the most interesting and potentially enlightening frontier. . . .

The Role of Chromosomes

Let's get back to Thomas and Patrick. Because it's unclear why twin brothers with identical genetic starting points and similar post-birth environments would take such divergent paths, it's helpful to return to the beginning.

Males and females have a fundamental genetic difference—females have two X chromosomes, and males have an X and a Y. Still, right after conception, it's hard to tell male and female zygotes apart, except for that tucked-away chromosomal difference. Normally, the changes take shape at a key point of fetal development, when the male brain is masculinized by sex hormones. The female brain is the default. The brain will stay on the female path as long as it is protected from exposure to hormones. The hormonal theory of homosexuality holds that, just as exposure to circulating sex hormones determines whether a fetus will be male or female, such exposure must also influence sexual orientation.

The cases of children born with disorders of "sexual differentiation" offer insight. William Reiner, a psychiatrist and urologist with the University of Oklahoma, has evaluated more than a hundred of these cases. For decades, the standard medical response to boys born with severely inadequate penises (or none at all) was to castrate the boy and have his parents raise him as a girl. But Reiner has found that nurture—even when it involves surgery soon after birth—cannot trump nature. Of the boys with inadequate penises who were raised as girls, he says, "I haven't found one who is sexually attracted to males." The majority of them have transitioned back to being males and report being attracted to females.

During fetal development, sexual identity is set before the sexual organs are formed, Reiner says. Perhaps it's the same for sexual orientation. In his research, of all the babies with X and Y chromosomes who were raised as girls, the only ones he has found who report having female identities and being attracted to males are those who did not have "receptors" to let the male sex hormones do their masculinizing in the womb.

The Role of Prenatal Biology

What does this all mean? "Exposure to male hormones in utero dramatically raises the chances of being sexually attracted to females," Reiner says. "We can infer that the absence of male hormone exposure may have something to do with attraction to males."

[Northwestern University psychologist] Michael Bailey says Reiner's findings represent a major breakthrough, showing that "whatever causes sexual orientation is strongly influenced by prenatal biology." Bailey and Reiner say the answer is probably not as simple as just exposure to sex hormones. After all, the exposure levels in some of the people Reiner studies are abnormal enough to produce huge differences in sexual organs. Yet, sexual organs in straight and gay people are, on average, the same. More likely, hormones are interacting with other factors.

Canadian researchers have consistently documented a "big-brother effect," finding that the chances of a boy being gay increase with each additional older brother he has. (Birth order does not appear to play a role with lesbians.) So, a male with

Study Based on Finger-Lengths

A California psychologist, Marc Breedlove, "conducted his research at three street fairs in the San Francisco Bay area in the fall of 1999." Each study participant had his or her hand photocopied on a portable copy machine to record finger length. Participants also filled out a questionnaire on sexual orientation and birth order. Seven hundred and twenty volunteers participated. They found that lesbians tended to have shorter index fingers (relative to their ring fingers) than did heterosexual women. They also found that gay males tended to have shorter index fingers (relative to their ring fingers) than heterosexual males. The relative size of a person's fingers is determined well before birth. These findings imply that sexual orientation is at least partly decided before birth—perhaps at conception when a person's unique DNA is established.

B.A. Robinson, "Six Studies into the Cause of Homosexuality," Ontario Consultants on Religious Tolerance, *updated March 12, 2006. www.religioustolerance.org.*

three older brothers is three times more likely to be gay than one with no older brothers, though there's still a better than 90 percent chance he will be straight. They argue that this results from a complex interaction involving hormones, antigens, and the mother's immune system.

By now, there is substantial evidence showing a correlation—though not causation—between sexual orientation and traits that are set when a baby is in the womb. Take finger length. In general, men have shorter index fingers in relation to their ring fingers; in women, the lengths are generally about the same. Researchers have found that lesbians generally have ratios closer to males. Other studies have shown masculinized results for lesbians in inner-ear functions and eye-blink reactions to sudden loud noises, and feminized patterns for gay men on certain cognitive tasks like spatial perception and remembering the placement of objects.

New York University researcher Lynn S. Hall, who has studied traits determined in the womb, speculates that Patrick was somehow prenatally stressed, probably during the first trimester, when the brain is really developing, particularly the structures like the hypothalamus that influence sexual behavior. This stress might have been based on his position in the womb or the blood flow to him or any of a number of other factors not in his mother's control. Yet more evidence that identical twins have womb experiences far from identical can be found in their often differing birth weights. Patrick was born a pound lighter than Thomas.

Taken together, the research suggests that early on in the womb as the fetus's brain develops in either the male or female direction, something fundamental to sexual orientation is happening. Nobody's sure what's causing it. But here's where genes may be involved, perhaps by regulating hormone exposure or by dictating the size of that key clump of neurons in the hypothalamus. Before researchers can sort that out, they'll need to return to the question of whether, in fact, there is a "gay gene." . . .

The Stakes Are High

In the course of reporting this story, I experienced a good deal of whiplash. Just when I would become swayed by the evidence supporting one discrete theory, I would stumble onto new evidence casting some doubt on it. Ultimately, I accepted this as unavoidable terrain in the hunt for the basis of sexual orientation. This is, after all, a research field built on underfunded, idiosyncratic studies that are met with full-barreled responses from opposing and well-funded advocacy groups determined to make the results from the lab hew to the scripts they've honed for the talk-show circuit.

You can't really blame the advocacy groups. The stakes are high. In the end, homosexuality remains such a divisive issue that only thoroughly tested research will get society to accept what science has to say about its origin. Critics of funding for sexual orientation research say that it isn't curing cancer, and they're right. But we devote a lot more dollars to studying other issues that aren't curing cancer and have less resonance in society.

Still, no matter how imperfect these studies are, when you put them all together and examine them closely, the message is clear: While post-birth development may well play a supporting role, the roots of homosexuality, at least in men, appear to be in place by the time a child is born. After spending years sifting through all the available data, British researchers Glenn Wilson and Qazi Rahman come to an even bolder conclusion in their forthcoming book *Born Gay: The Psychobiology of Sex Orientation*, in which they write: "Sexual orientation is something we are born with and not 'acquired' from our social environment."

Meanwhile, the mother of twins Patrick and Thomas has done her own sifting and has come to her own conclusions. She says her son's feminine behavior suggests he will grow up to be gay, and she has no problem with that. She just worries about what happens to him between now and then.

Patrick's Future

After that fateful call from Patrick's school, she says, "I knew I had to talk to my son, and I had no clue what to say." Ultimately, she told him that although he could play however he wanted at home, he couldn't tell his classmates he was a girl, because they'd think he was lying. And she told him that some older boys might be mean to him and even hit him if he continued to claim he was a girl.

Then she asked him, "Do you think that you can convince yourself that you are a boy?"

"Yes, Mom," he said. "It's going to be like when I was trying to learn to read, and then one day I opened the book and I could read."

His mother's heart sank. She could tell that he wanted more than anything to please her. "Basically, he was saying there must be a miracle—that one day I wake up and I'm a boy. That's the only way he could imagine it could happen."

In the year since that conversation, Patrick's behavior has become somewhat less feminine. His mother hopes it's just because his interests are evolving and not because he's suppressing them.

"I can now imagine him being completely straight, which I couldn't a year ago," she says. "I can imagine him being gay, which seems to be statistically most likely."

She says she's fine with either outcome, just as long as he's happy and free from harm. She takes heart in how much more accepting today's society is. "By the time my boys are 20, the world will have changed even more."

By then, there might even be enough consensus for researchers to forget about finger lengths and fruit flies and gay sheep, and move on to a new mystery.

VIEWPOINT 3

"The most common conflicts . . . that predispose individuals to homosexual attractions and behaviors are loneliness and sadness, profound feelings of inadequacy, mistrust and fear, narcissism, sexual addiction, excessive anger, sexual abuse in childhood and a lack of balance in one's life."

Homosexuality Is Caused by Psychological Trauma

Richard Fitzgibbons

In the following viewpoint, Dr. Richard Fitzgibbons argues that, in many cases, homosexuality arises as a result of psychological events that influence people when they are young. A child's relationship with unloving or unsupportive parents, or an experience of sexual abuse, can disrupt the normal process of sexual development, the author contends. Ultimately, excessive anger or narcissism, the viewpoint concludes, is a powerful factor in leading to homosexuality. Dr. Richard Fitzgibbons is a psychiatrist and director of Comprehensive Counseling Services in W. Conshohocken, Pennsylvania, and the co-author of "Helping Clients Forgive: An Empirical Guide."

Richard Fitzgibbons, "Origin and Healing of Homosexual Attractions and Behaviors," *Catholic Education Resource Center*, May 1996.

As you read, consider the following questions:

1. How does sexual addiction resemble substance abuse disorders, according to the author?
2. As argued by Fitzgibbons, how can a weak masculine identity contribute to the rise of homosexuality?
3. According to the viewpoint, why is narcissism and selfishness linked to the homosexual lifestyle?

The most common conflicts at different life stages that predispose individuals to homosexual attractions and behavior are loneliness and sadness, profound feelings of inadequacy, mistrust and fear, narcissism, sexual addiction, excessive anger, sexual abuse in childhood and a lack of balance in one's life. During times of stress these inner difficulties are activated. In an attempt to seek relief or to escape from this unconscious emotional pain, strong sexual temptations and behavior can occur. This dynamic of inner emotional suffering leading to homosexual desires and activity rarely can begin during childhood but usually it develops in early adolescence. However, adult life may be the first time for the emergence of this disorder.

Sadness and Loneliness

The most frequently seen cause of sadness in the past leading to homosexual attractions in males was the result of childhood and adolescent rejection by peers because of very limited athletic abilities. More recently, the collapse of the nuclear family with almost 40 percent of children and teenagers living apart from their fathers has resulted in serious problems with sadness and loneliness in our young. The failure to receive warmth, affection, and praise from a mother can result also in a terrible inner emptiness and sadness. Some females will attempt to fill this void for gentle, comforting maternal love through homosexual behavior.

Weak Masculine Identity

Another important cause of homosexual temptations and acting-out behavior is the result of strong feelings of insecurity. A lack of confidence may arise from rejection by parents, peers, siblings and other significant people in whom one wanted to invest trust. In an unconscious attempt to undo the earlier life rejection, a person may seek validation and acceptance from members of the same sex. In my clinical experience this painful emotional conflict is seen much more frequently in males.

However, the most common early life disappointments leading to homosexual desires is the result of peer rejections because of a boy's poor eye-hand and athletic coordination. This is a very difficult weakness to have in a culture that is obsessed with successful athletic performance to the point where it is seen as the major measure of masculinity. Children who are not athletically coordinated are regularly the last to be chosen to join teams and are often the victims of rejection and ridicule. They are referred to regularly in a feminine manner through the use of such painful names as sissy, fairy, and queer. Also, they may be told that they run or act like a girl. As the betrayal pain by their peers continues year after year, these males feel increasingly inadequate, confused, isolated, lonely, and weak. This harsh treatment by peers results in these youngsters having a very poor body image and a poor sense of their masculinity.

Fear and Mistrust

Fear of vulnerability to heterosexual relationships is another important factor in the development of homosexual attractions. This inability to feel safe loving someone of the opposite sex is usually unconscious and originates most often from traumatic experiences within the home. In males, this may be a consequence of having a mother who was overly controlling, excessively needy or dependent, angry and critical, unaffectionate and cold, narcissistic and insensitive, very mistrustful and addicted or ill. In females, the fear of trusting males in a loving relationship may arise from having a father who was very angry, rejecting and distant, insensitive toward the mother, abusive, harsh, selfish, addicted or unloving. Today, abandonment pain by the father from divorce is one of the major sources of male mistrust in females who develop an unconscious dread of being hurt as they saw their mothers wounded by their fathers. Subsequently, such females for a period of time may only feel safe being comforted in love by another female.

Sexual Addiction

The sexually compulsive, highly reckless, and life-threatening behavior in a large percentage of homosexuals would indicate the presence of an addictive disorder in these individuals. These addictions resemble substance abuse disorders in that individuals engage in compulsive behaviors that are medically hazardous.

This clinical view of much homosexual behavior as being addictive in nature is supported by numerous studies of the sexual practices of homosexuals and by the recent best estimates that one half of all homosexual males in New York City are HIV positive. The National Institutes of Health [NIH] estimated that at current rates of infection, a majority of twenty year old gay or bisexual men nationwide will eventually have the AIDS virus. . . . The addictive nature of much homosexual behavior explains why HIV infections have quadrupled in San Francisco since 1987.

These studies support the clinical view that homosexuality is a disorder with extremely compulsive, highly reckless, and self-destructive features.

Narcissism

Narcissism or selfishness is another major factor influencing the attraction to the homosexual lifestyle. The appeal here is

The Feelings Behind SSA

In May and June 2004, People Can Change surveyed the members of its online support groups, which have a combined total membership of about 600 men—all of whom are seeking to overcome unwanted homosexual feelings (or feelings of "same-sex attraction," or SSA). The survey sought to determine what biological and environmental factors the members of People Can Change believe contributed to the development of their SSA feelings. A total of 205 surveys were completed—a response rate of 34%. . . .

This summary ranks their responses in a variety of ways, but the most frequently cited responses were:

1. **Relationship with or feelings about their father:** 97% said this was a contributing factor in their development of same-sex attractions, and 71% said it was one of the three most significant factors.
2. **Relationship with or feelings about their male peers:** Again, 97% said this was a contributing factor, while 49% said it was one of the "top three" factors.
3. **Relationship with or feelings about their mother:** 91% said this was a contributing factor, and 36% said it was one of the three most significant factors.

"Factors Contributing to the Development of Their Homosexual Feelings," People Can Change, 2004. www.peoplecanchange.com.

multifaceted and includes not having to make a total commitment to one person and not having to give oneself completely as a parent. There is a desire to remain childlike with minimal obligations in relationships and few limitations to the pursuit of pleasure. Hedonism is associated with many people involved in the homosexual behavior.

Attempt to Flee from an Excessive Sense of Responsibility

Some people attempt to escape from excessive pressures and burdens by engaging in homosexual activities in which there is no commitment, obligation, or responsibility. Married men sometimes struggle with intense insecurity after experiencing the stress of a negative boss, a lack of success in work, or a sense of overwhelming anxiety from financial worries. Then they began to view their wives and children as burdens and difficulties rather than as gifts from God. They engage in homosexual behavior in an attempt to flee from their stress and to feel more lovable and special.

Sexual Trauma in Childhood

A number of males who were raped or sexually abused by older males in childhood develop confusion about their masculine identity. As with other victims of rape, they think that their behavior must have in some way led to the abuse. Such traumatic experiences can create self-hatred and the false belief that they must be homosexual. As adolescents, their relationship with girls is often undermined by their shame and the belief that no female could possibly love them it they knew of their sexual experiences.

Anger

The most significant type of anger influencing the development of homosexual attractions in childhood is anger with oneself. As a result of ongoing rejections by peers, many boys acquire an intense dislike for their bodies and view them as weak, unattractive, and unmasculine. They are so uncomfortable with their physiques that it is not unusual for them to spend a great deal of time fantasizing about escaping from their own bodies by assuming the body of another. This daydreaming can begin when they are very young and may lead to a strong physical attraction for those of the same sex.

Finally, excessive anger is seen in a number of other areas in the homosexual lifestyle. Most importantly, passive-aggressive anger, which is the quiet venting of hostility while pretending not to be angry, is manifested in the failure of HIV-positive individuals to inform their sexual partners of their illness. These men and women often feel that since they have to suffer, others should also. Intense anger is also seen in homosexuals within the media or in the educational, political, ministerial and mental health fields when they attempt to force our culture to change its views on homosexuality. Their approaches are often direct assaults against Judeo-Christian morality, the nuclear family, and the basic differences between men and women.

Viewpoint 4

"All of these attempts to label us only encourage others to look at us as something less than human."

The Causes of Homosexuality Are Irrelevant

Andrew Fink

In the following viewpoint, Andrew Fink argues that attempts to explain the cause of homosexuality are hurtful. Both religious arguments that condemn homosexuality because of biblical injunctions and scientific inquiries that try to identify biological causes ignore individuality and personhood, the author contends. He concludes that any attempt to define people or to give them labels is bigotry.

Fink, a gay man, has written articles, poetry, and fiction for the Web site Helium.com, an online community of freelance writers, on topics including race, sexual orientation, and chemistry.

As you read, consider the following questions:

1. What biblical quotation does the author cite to demonstrate the arguments of the Christian right?

Andrew Fink, "Deliberations on the Cause of Homosexuality," www.helium.com., 2008. Reproduced by permission.

2. According to the viewpoint, what does the Stockholm Brain Institute offer as a contributing factor to sexual orientation?
3. What does the author say he has gained from being gay?

Every once in a while, as I read the paper, I will come across another study on homosexuality. Usually it's some Institute peeling apart brains of gay men and women, looking for something different. Always something different. I read it, even though I don't want to. Even though I feel like I am being placed under a microscope, being scrutinized for the simple fact that I love a man. I go on the Internet, and then I am barraged by some other argument, usually the Pope or a minister in Colorado Springs, accusing homosexuality of creating every problem in the world, or claiming that it is Satan manifested upon the earth. I might read that too, but usually I get about halfway before I become so disgusted I give up. And all of this leaves me wondering why I need an excuse for the way I am. No one should have to justify his or her thoughts. People should simply learn to accept differences, and move on. Drop it. Moot point. Irrelevant. Isn't that why our society was founded? Freedom of thought and all that jazz? People just can't stop fighting over what causes sexuality. Is it biology or childhood? Nature or nurture? Bigotry or bigotry is the way I see it. Both sides are trying to uphold equally debasing positions that leave people like me feeling that these excuses are simply another attempt to make me conform to their world view.

Religious Arguments Are Hurtful

At least one side knows that they're trumpeting bigotry. Many in the Christian right hurl biblical bombs from afar, lashing out with quotes such as, Levictus 18:22: "You shall not lie with a male as with a woman; it is an abomination." This message, at least, is clear. Hurtful and hateful, but clear. I don't think they understand their arguments very well, or, what they think are arguments, but are generally broad claims about how gays are hurting civilization, or the family. They depict gays as monsters trying to dismantle everything that our society holds dear. I admit, if I met a gay person like that, I wouldn't like them either. I don't think anyone would. But we aren't like that, or at least, I'm not. And my gay friends aren't. Generalizations aren't going to get us anywhere but hurt. We are people first, and gays second. The right wants people to forget that. To them, we are only gays. Not even human, just odd figures dressed in leather and drag, dancing through the streets of San Francisco or Amsterdam, corrupting children with our pornography and massive pelvic thrusts.

I don't much like that aspect of gay culture either. I don't understand it; I don't personally feel like dancing through the streets. In some ways, it disgusts me. I don't know why a guy would want to dress up as a woman, just because he likes men, or because he thinks he's a woman. It's confusing, a little creepy, but whatever. Some people do, I can deal with that. I'm not an activist either. I'm not about to start waving a big rainbow flag around campus, thinking I can make the world change in a day, or protest by protest. To me, any discrimination that is challenged is already dying. I am content to wait it out. Everyone's yelling and screaming can't hide the fact that the Christian right doesn't have a sound argument other than the Bible. And, as much as they wish it were, our nation isn't founded on the Bible. It's founded on the Constitution, and I think that document will pull through for us in the end. Christians don't have to like me, but when they think that not liking me gives them the right to restrict my rights, they've gone too far. I will love whom I will love. There's not much I can do about that.

Science Offers No Comfort

The left wants to help though. They think it's important to protect my rights, and that's fine. I like having my rights being protected. But they aren't taking a very good approach to protect me. They just raise walls of scientific studies such as Simon Levay's research in the seventies, or the more recent study from the Stockholm Brain Institute, which states that, "The important thing is to be open to the likely situation that there are biological factors that contribute to sexual orientation." While much friendlier, it is scathing for another, subtler, reason. I took psychology in high school. The reason I took it was to learn more about who I was becoming. I was scared of myself, of my feelings, and I wanted to learn more about homosexuality. Needless to say, I learned a lot. Behaviorists think that homosexuality is just a ploy people put on to gain attention. Others think that the chance of being a homosexual is increased by the number of older brothers one has. Others think boys fall in love with their father's penis, or girls adore their mother's vagina. Maybe it's faulty memory in the brain, a chemical imbalance, or repressed childhood trauma. But what does any of this mean to me? It sounds like, to me, there must be something wrong with me. Like homosexuality is no better than a disease, or something that can be cured with a positive mental outlook. It can't. I tried fixing myself for about six years. It didn't help. I know people who try for longer than that, who keep hidden hoping no one will notice. But there's nothing wrong with us. I'm a person, no one can deny that. I can't be reduced to racing electrical impulses, or hormonal imbalances, or a collection of memories and learned responses to environmental stimuli. I may have a brain, but I am beyond that brain. Just as I am not a leather and drag monster, I'm not a little puzzle that can be taken apart and solved again, placing the missing piece of sexuality into its correct spot.

Both of these sides are saying the same thing in different forms, that homosexuality is something bad, something wrong. An abnormality, a defect, a flaw. Both use a source of ultimate knowledge to offer empirical evidence that supports their claims, and both hurt, more than help homosexuality. Anyone can see this is the intent of the former. To the Christian right,

Science Cannot Settle This Question

[M]edicine, which is what we rely on to tell us what is "healthy," will always seek to change the way peoples' bodies and minds and hearts work; yesterday's immutable state of nature is tomorrow's disease to be cured. Medical science can only take its cues from the society whose curiosities it satisfies and whose confusions it investigates. It can never do the heavy political lifting required to tell us whether one way of living our lives is better than another. This is exactly why [nineteenth-century writer Karoly Maria] Kertbeny originated the notion of a biologically based sexual orientation, and, to the extent that society is more tolerant of homosexuality now than it was 150 years ago, that idea has been a success. But the ex-gay movement may be the signal that this invention has begun to outlive its usefulness, that sexuality, profoundly mysterious and irrational, will not be contained by our categories, that it is time to find reasons other than medical science to insist that people ought to be able to love whom they love.

Gary Greenberg,
"Gay by Choice?" Mother Jones,
September-October 2007, pp. 61–65, 93–94.

we are simply immoral, perverse sinners blind to the redeeming hand of God. They create organizations such as Love in Action (loveinaction.org) to restore "those trapped in sexual and relational sin through the power of Jesus Christ." But the left, how could that ever be seen as bigotry? Certainly they are doing their best to protect and support my lifestyle? They're just trying to help me, I'm sure. However, all of their scientific studies scream, "Don't hate them! They can't help it!" As if there's something to be helped.

My Differences Don't Define Me

I like being gay. To be honest, it's one of the best things that ever happened to me. It has opened my eyes to so much difference in the world, something most people try to glaze over. I respect differences because I am different. I may be quiet about it; I'm not going to tell random people I'm gay just to gauge their reactions. I don't care if they like me. I might not like them either. But my differences shouldn't define who I am. I am not a gay student; I am a student who happens to be gay. It's circumstantial; it doesn't matter to me, why does it matter to everyone else so damn much?

The simple truth is, it shouldn't matter what causes homosexuality. What does matter is that all of these attempts to label us only encourage others to look at us as something less than human. Something other. I already know one side sees me like that, something to be feared, hated and destroyed. The other side doesn't know it, but as they sit upon their almighty pedestal of biology, they are sweeping the rug of humanity right out from under my feet. They want to know what makes me tick? Well, I don't know why I am the way I am, but I'll tell you who I am. I'm a human being. Just like you. Just like that person sitting across from you on the busy bus sipping that Starbucks coffee and reading the paper. Some people seem to have forgotten. I just have a different approach to life.

Oh wait, doesn't everybody? That's what makes our society great. We can live our lives as we choose. Without labels, without definitions, but most importantly, without judgments. I could condemn the left's dependency on science, but I won't. I could sling hate back at the Christians who hate me for whom I love, but I won't. Because they don't deserve to feel how they have made me feel. No one does. So, why do they all insist on making me feel hated? Why do they insist I am something less than human, something to be examined, something to be feared, something to be fixed? If they don't need an excuse for their behavior, then neither should I, nor, for that matter, anyone else. But if it keeps up, I may start asking for funding. It's about time someone discovers the bigotry gene.

Viewpoint 5

> *"I felt gay, and thought I wanted to live my life that way, but I found a way out."*

Homosexuality Can Be "Cured"

"Ben Newman" [pseudonym]

In the following viewpoint, "Ben Newman" tells the story of his own treatment with a therapist and his recovery from a life of homosexual sex addiction. Contrary to the conclusions of the American Psychological Association, the author argues, sexual orientation can be changed through psychotherapy, and he himself is living proof. "Ben Newman" and all of the other names in the following viewpoint are pseudonyms created by the author, who keeps his real name secret to protect his family's privacy. He is a public relations professional and webmaster for the Web site PeopleCanChange.com.

As you read, consider the following questions:

1. How long had the author been living a double life before he sought treatment, according to the viewpoint?
2. As the author tells it, how did the high priests of his church respond when he confessed his sins to them?

"Ben Newman" [pseudonym], "Change of Heart: My Two Years in Reparative Therapy," *NARTH*, September 20, 2004. Reproduced by permission.

3. How long did the author's therapy with Matt last, as related in the viewpoint?

In May 1997, I was in a complete state of crisis as I entered reparative therapy for homosexual sex addiction. My wife had caught me in yet another lie that was supposed to cover up my double life. Surely, this would be the last straw. Surely, this time she would leave me and never come back, taking our two beautiful children with her. I was completely panicked.

Entering the therapist's office for the first time caused me no particular discomfort; my panic over my marriage eclipsed any nervousness I might have had about what might happen in therapy.

I had met my new therapist, "Matt," just six weeks earlier through a self-help group for men who struggle with unwanted homosexual desires. He had impressed me with two things: his youthful attractiveness and masculine appearance—with eyes that seemed to peer into my soul—and the fact that he reported that he had once dealt with homosexual longings himself but had resolved them.

The latter fact gave me great confidence and hope. I had read the writings of people who made the generic claim that "others have come out of homosexuality, so you can too," but nothing I had read actually identified who these so-called former homosexuals were, and for years I had doubted their existence. Matt was the first real live human being I had ever met who said, "I felt gay, and thought I wanted to live my life that way, but I found a way out that gave me more happiness and peace by healing than indulging." I didn't know what that meant, exactly, but I trusted that he, more than anyone else I had ever met, could help me find a way out of the pit I was in.

And a very deep pit it was. I was living a complete double life. Happy husband and father, church-goer and successful professional on the outside, rabid homosexual sex addict on the inside. After 14 years of this pattern, I had surrendered myself to it, convinced that I was going to have to live my life this way, somehow hoping the inside and outside never collided and destroyed my life.

Now, as I entered the therapists' offices, my hidden life was in fact on a direct collision course with my false front. I could see my life about to fall down around me. Suicide was becoming an increasingly appealing option.

The APA's Disclaimer

The first order of business on my first visit with Matt was for me to sign a Consent to Treat form. It was required by the clinic, as a result of the American Psychological Association's [APA's] resolutions which discourage this type of treatment. Reparative therapy was unproven, the form said; the APA's official stance was that it didn't believe it was possible to change sexual orientation; attempting to do so might even cause psychological harm.

Yeah, right, I thought, as if the double life I was living was not causing psychological harm enough.

Too, I resented the suggestion that the only "correct" solution (politically correct, anyway) for me was to abandon my wife and children and throw myself into the gay life. That was not what I wanted. I had had the chance to do that before I met Diane and had children with her, when the stakes were much lower—and I realized then that that was not what I wanted. While dating men, adopting a gay identity, and throwing myself into the gay lifestyle had been exhilarating at first, it had soon felt like it was killing my spirit, alienating myself from my goals in life, from God and a sense of higher purpose. I had realized then that I didn't want to be affirmed as gay; I wanted to be affirmed as a man.

But throughout the early years of our marriage, unable to find significant help in dealing with the homosexual struggles that still raged just below the surface, I had resorted to a horrific double life. Until I met Matt, I had given up all hope that I could ever change. Right now, it felt like Matt was my only hope.

In our first session, I blurted out the whole story with a frankness and abandon that was unprecedented for me. Matt was safe to tell. I didn't have to worry about seeking his approval or about there being any consequences in my life for divulging my story to him. He responded with candor: "Your life is a mess." I was surprised at his bluntness, but knew it to be true. "I can help you work through the immediate crisis," he said, "but unless you go a whole lot deeper than that, you'll just go back out there and delay the inevitable recurrence—probably with even greater consequences next time."

I agreed. I had hit bottom. I was ready to do whatever it took to salvage the mess of my life. Over the next several weeks, I practically ran to Matt's office each Tuesday evening, finding a place of safety and solace where I could get help and guidance with the darkest secrets of my life. I grieved with him over the intense pain I had caused my wife and her very legitimate hurt and rage at me. How relieved I was that, seeing my resolve to work with Matt and with hope in this new resource, she tentatively decided not to leave—at least not yet.

Uncovering the Wounds

My next crisis was to prepare myself to make a full confession to the high priests of my church, where I served as a lay elder. I knew I would never make a permanent change if I continued to hide my secret life from them, and I had committed to Diane that I would do so, as a condition of her staying with me. But coming clean to these men—men of authority, men I feared would reject me—was the most terrifying thing I could imagine. Yet when I did, they responded with kindness and concern. Still, they could not tolerate that kind of sexual behavior from a church elder. They decided to excommunicate me and give me the opportunity to be re-baptized a year later, with a fresh start, as long as I proved myself able to remain faithful to my wife for at least a year and demonstrated a credible commitment to remain faithful to her thereafter.

My excommunication was handled without trying to humiliate me. I was still welcome to attend meetings as an unbaptized guest, and my status as an excommunicant was not publicly known among the general membership of the church. Nevertheless, the whole experience stirred up intense feelings of rejection and shame. The floodgates opened, and in therapy Matt and I explored a lifetime of perceived rejection from men. In successive therapy sessions, I cried and I raged.

To my amazement, Matt encouraged the full expression of this anger in my sessions with him. But I wanted to freeze up instead, paralyzed with fear and shame. Wasn't anger bad? I thought. Wasn't it out of control? Good boys don't get mad. And worst of all, what might I uncover just underneath the paralysis? But Matt taught me it was this hidden anger and shame, in part, that I was turning on myself self-destructively and that was driving me to act out sexually. The anger needed to be expressed legitimately. It needed to be honored.

He tried to teach me how to express it, to feel it in my body. I couldn't get it. I felt like a grade school student grappling with a graduate school problem. What was he pushing me to do? Finally, he explained it in a language I could understand: "It's like phone sex, but with anger instead of sex." Oh! I laughed, why didn't you say that before!

And so the anger spilled out of me: anger at my father for being emotionally checked out of my life; rage at Mike the Bully for his constant ridicule of me in high school; rage at my mother for shaming me over my maleness; hurt that I had been carrying around inside of me my whole life, where it could continue to attack me from within. With Matt coaching me, I visualized fighting back, ejecting the taunts, shame and rejection from my heart, and then destroying them. Over the months we repeated this process, until at last I could find no

The Formation of "Ex-gay" Groups

An interesting development followed the APA's [American Psychiatric Association's] decision in 1973 [to declassify homosexuality as a disorder] and a companion move by the American Psychological Association. Looking for therapeutic help that was no longer available, men in the process of changing their orientation began to set up support groups to help each other. Late in the seventies, they began to join forces and to proliferate. There are now at least 150 of these groups in the United States, Europe, South East Asia, and Australia. They came to be known for a while as "ex-gay" groups—the largest being a confederation of groups called Exodus International. Few of them like the word "ex-gay" however, and have actively sought alternatives, none of which has generally caught-on. . . .

Exodus is basically Protestant. Smaller groups have other affiliations: Evergreen (Mormon), Courage (Roman Catholic), Jonah (Jewish). No group had emerged by 2007 within the Islamic community though there are definite stirrings of interest.

Neil Whitehead and Briar Whitehead,
"Can You Change Your Sexual Orientation?"
My Genes Made Me Do It—
A Scientific Look at Sexual Orientation, *1999.*
Last updated Feb. 2008. www.mygenes.co.nz.

more anger stirring within me. At last, having emptied a lifetime of pent-up anger from my wounded soul, I was ready to release and forgive.

At other times, Matt worked with me on my addictive cycles. We explored in depth what seemed to trigger my acting out—stress, anger, fear, almost any uncomfortable emotion caused me to try to seek solace in the arms of men and the drug-like rush of forbidden sexual stimulation. I determined to return to Sexaholics Anonymous, where I had once started to make progress toward breaking my addictive cycles. As I did, and as I processed my emotional life in depth with Matt each week, the cycles first slowed and then tapered off dramatically.

Entering the World of Men

Matt taught me about defensive detachment, and I learned how I had defensively rejected men in order to protect myself from being hurt by them. I pored over a book by Dr. Joseph Nicolosi, called *Reparative Therapy of Male Homosexuality*, and was amazed to find my exact psychological profile, it seemed—complete with defensive detachment as described in his book.

Matt helped me open my mind and heart to the possibility of finding a heterosexual man or men whom I could turn to for help and support throughout my week. It was terrifying, but I approached Mark, a man at my church about eight years older than I, and asked him to be a spiritual mentor to me. He readily agreed. He knew nothing about homosexuality, but he knew about God, and he knew about pain, and he was more than willing to be there for me. I talked with him at least weekly, sometimes several times a week, baring my soul. I called him when I was tempted to act out. I called him when I stumbled, and he helped lift me back up.

Matt's joy for me in my newfound friendship was palpable. "I wish I could meet him!" he said. "Heck, I wish I could clone him for my other clients!"

This was something I had come to love about Matt—for all his unvarnished candor about my mistakes and self-destructive blunders, I felt his authentic joy in my successes and growth. I was truly coming to love this man as a brother in a way I had never loved a brother in my life.

Still, there were plenty of times I froze in fear at the prospect of reaching out to other men in friendship. I was convinced that heterosexual men didn't have friends—didn't even need friends. Their wives or girlfriends were supposed to be enough for them. Certainly, my father never had any friends, and never went anywhere socially without my mother. I could only remember one friend that my three much-older brothers had between them. How could I rely on heterosexual men to be there for me, to be my friends, to meet my needs for male companionship and affirmation? I had always believed the only men who wanted anything to do with other men were gay.

Matt challenged me to open my eyes, to look beyond my engrained perceptions. "Your soul demands male connection, and that desire WILL express itself, one way or another. It WILL come out. Suppressing it will only work for a short while, and then the dam will burst. If you don't experience authentic, intimate male connection platonically, the need will absolutely drive you to find it sexually. One way or another, the need will be met."

The words resonated within me: One way or another, the need will be met. I knew it was true for me. I pushed myself to reach out of my shell. I started observing heterosexual men more. I started to notice men going out to eat together, going to the movies together, going to men's groups, working on cars together. At parties, I noticed the men cluster in groups separate from the women within moments of arriving. They hung out together watching a game on TV as they talked, or playing pool, or some other activity.

I was discovering the world of men as if for the first time. I would come into a therapy session with Matt and share my discoveries with him as I sought to understand and demystify the world of men. We talked about the things that men do, how they are at parties, how they are with each other and with women. I started to understand them, then appreciate them—then, a bit at a time, to feel that I wasn't so different from them. . . .

In February 1999, having been faithful to Diane for a year and a half and feeling like I had grown enough and healed enough now to renew my commitments to her and my church, I was baptized in a small and beautiful ceremony. Mark, Rob, and other friends from our church were there. Diane was there with tears in her eyes, glowing with pride and relief that I had "come home." Later, as I shared my feelings about the experience with Matt, he mirrored my joy in the huge step this was in my life and how far I had come. . . .

My Own Man

I walked out of Matt's office for the last time on August 25, 1999, twenty-seven months after I had first walked in. I was a different man. Stronger. Happier. More grounded. Whole. I had been "sexually sober" and faithful to my wife for two years—and had found peace and joy in doing so.

As I left the last session, I hugged Matt firmly, burying my head into his chest. "I love you," I told him. "I'll never forget what you've done for me." With tears in his eyes, he said, "I love you too." If only I could keep him as a friend, always. But something inside of me told me: "Friendship is forever. Even if you can't be his friend in this life, you will be in the next. This powerful bond between you will be forever."

And perhaps more important, I would take the gifts he had given me with me into every other relationship from now on. I didn't need Matt as a therapist any more, because now I could be in honest relationships with others. I could make friends. I could ask for help. I could be real.

And more than anything else, I could love. I had learned to give love and receive love from other men as my brothers, and trust them with my heart. In this, I truly had found what I had been looking for all my life.

"There is simply no sufficiently scientifically sound evidence that sexual orientation can be changed."

Homosexuality Cannot Be "Cured"

Casey Sanchez

In the following viewpoint, journalist Casey Sanchez analyzes programs that seek to "cure" homosexual people of the sin and the disease of same-sex attraction. Sanchez argues that the so-called ex-gay movement, although it intends to offer help to struggling people, actually causes serious psychological damage. He contends that the movement errs by convincing gays and lesbians that something is wrong with them, rather than by helping them accept who they are. Sanchez is a staff journalist for the Intelligence Report *at the Southern Poverty Law Center in Montgomery, Alabama, where he specializes in writing about bigotry and racism.*

As you read, consider the following questions:

1. Why were clients of the Love in Action program forbidden to talk with their families, according to the author?

Casey Sanchez, "Straight Like Me," *Intelligence Report*, Winter 2007, pp. 48–55.

2. As the viewpoint describes it, what is the purpose of the Box Turtle Bulletin?
3. How large is the membership of NARTH (the National Association for Research and Therapy of Homosexuality), according to the viewpoint?

John Smid has a high school diploma, a minister's license and five acres of land outside Memphis, Tenn., where he "cures" homosexuals. For most of the past two decades, Smid's residential "ex-gay" program was known as Love in Action [LIA]. The majority of the young men who entered the program came from the kind of conservative religious upbringing where being gay is a sin that will cast a person out of church, family and home. To rid themselves of "unwanted same-sex attractions" they paid $1,000 a month, with some staying at the facility for years.

At LIA, as it was known, staff would lead clients in group sessions to trace out childhood trauma alongside lessons in throwing footballs, changing motor oil and learning how to cross their legs in a manly fashion. In much of the world of ex-gay ministries, same-sex attractions are thought to result from childhood sexual abuse or parents who failed to instill masculinity in their sons. Since the goal is to rewire parent-child dynamics, LIA clients were forbidden to call their families. Those who worked in Memphis while living on the LIA compound had to navigate around a "forbidden zone" that covered nearly half the city, keeping them miles away from its handful of adult book stores. They were ordered to drive straight to and from work without speaking to strangers.

"On our way to work, we saw two cars get into an accident. We actually debated over whether we should stop," said Peterson Toscano, who lived at LIA for two years in the early 1990s and now helms an ex-gay survivors' movement. They didn't stop. "Looking back, I see how brainwashed we were. We were sick the whole day. We could have helped the people."

Toscano still has the 374–page LIA handbook that governed every day he spent trying to become heterosexual. Tom Otteson, another former client of Smid's, said he was told that "it would be better if I were to commit suicide than go back into the world and become a homosexual again." In 2005, Smid tried to clarify those comments to a reporter from the pro-gay Memphis magazine *Family & Friends*: "I said [to Otteson], 'It would almost be better if you weren't alive than to return back to the life that you have struggled so much to leave.'"

Unlike his clients, Smid was not isolated from the world. In 2005, when Tennessee officials investigated LIA for dispensing psychotropic medicine and treating minors without a license, it seemed certain the place would be shut down. But Smid kept his operation alive by countersuing the state of Tennessee with the help of senior counsel from the Alliance Defense Fund, the powerhouse legal arm of the Christian right.

Today, Love in Action is part of a booming phenomenon that is also known as the "sexual reorientation therapy" movement, an effort that is reflected in the hundreds of programs attached to religious organizations across the United States. Although the stated aim of the movement is to turn gays straight and bring them to God, it actually now has as much to do with battling the gay rights movement by trying to prove that sexuality is not an immutable characteristic like race or gender. Ex-gay ministries began as redoubts for men and women trying to reconcile their faith and sexuality. But in the hands of the anti-gay Christian right, they have become full-fledged propaganda machines depicting gays as sex-addicted, mentally ill, and stunted heterosexuals. . . .

"New Creations"?

Reparative or sexual reorientation therapy, the pseudo-scientific foundation of the ex-gay movement, has been discredited by virtually all major American medical, psychiatric, psychological and professional counseling organizations. The American Psychological Association, for instance, declared in 2006: "There is simply no sufficiently scientifically sound evidence that sexual orientation can be changed. Our further concern is that the positions espoused by NARTH [the National Association for Research & Therapy of Homosexuality] and Focus on the Family create an environment in which prejudice and discrimination can flourish." The powerful American Medical Association, for its part, officially "opposes the use of 'reparative' or 'conversion' therapy that is based on the assumption that homosexuality per se is a mental disorder or based upon the a priori assumption that the patient should change his/her homosexual orientation."

Nevertheless, over the past three decades, ex-gay ministries have developed a storyline where men and women can become "new creations" in Christ, adopting a heterosexual identity even if they never completely rid themselves of their homosexual attractions.

Jim Burroway, who runs Box Turtle Bulletin, a Web site that tracks the ex-gay movement, says a key theme in ex-gay ideology is the idea that "there's no such thing as gay:" Instead, gays and lesbians are described as "sexually broken" or heterosexuals who suffer from "same-sex attractions."

Sexual brokenness, according to ex-gay doctrine, usually occurs early in childhood, the result of an overbearing mother, an emotionally distant father, or sexual abuse. Focus on the Family ex-gay lecturers routinely and flatly declare that *all* gays and lesbians are victims of childhood sexual abuse.

About the only time the word "gay" appears in the ex-gay lexicon is in the phrase "gay lifestyle," which is largely seen as describing a hedonistic mix of one-night stands and sexually transmitted diseases that culminates in early death or abandonment when youthful beauty fades. The ex-gay movement has little language to describe the real world in which lesbians and gays hold elected office, appear on TV shows and raise families. At best, people like U.S. Rep. Barney Frank (D-Mass.) and talk show host Ellen DeGeneres are labeled as "gay-identified." Exodus president Alan Chambers and other, harsher ex-gay leaders call them "militant gays," simply because they are not actively working to renounce their same-sex attractions. Churches that accept gays are branded "false churches."

Still, even many ex-gay proponents admit that total conversion to heterosexuality is at best an elusive goal. Frank Worthen, who runs the ex-gay residential program New Hope out of an apartment complex in San Rafael, [California], writes in his curriculum workbook *Steps Out*: "Our primary goal is not to make heterosexuals out of homosexual people. God alone determines whether a former homosexual person is to marry and rear a family, or if he (or she) is to remain celibate, serving the Lord with his whole heart."

"Ancestor Sin" and 40-Day Fasts

Exodus, which has a $1 million budget, and NARTH both provide referrals to ex-gay programs and therapists that offer a bewildering array of techniques and philosophies. . . .

Exodus makes referrals to ministries like Living Waters, a popular neo-Pentecostal ex-gay program that treats homosexuality as a spirit that can be induced by "ancestor sin" and pushed out through exorcism. "We had pretty much a whole day dedicated to going through our entire genealogy and asking for forgiveness for the sins of our ancestors," said Eric Leocadio, who went through the 30-week program in his early 20s. He says he was also told to keep "certain boundaries in your friendship, never connecting with someone emotionally because you might fall in love with them."

During his time with Living Waters, Toscano said a pastor had him fast for a week at a time. "He said it was a matter of breaking through physical appetites related to lust. . . . There were others who fasted, sometimes for up to 40 days."

Secular ex-gay therapies, even if less physically demanding, are no less bizarre. On Ex-Gay Watch, a watchdog Web site, a woman named Pamela Ferguson describes the reparative therapy her ex-husband underwent as a last-ditch attempt to save their marriage. "I was once told to hold [my ex-husband's] penis in my hand as we fell asleep. After a week or two of this, [he supposedly] would be suddenly and inexplicably inflamed with desire for me." The couple declined the suggestion.

At "ex-gay barbecues" held at her house, Ferguson says she met several men who said they were asked to measure their penises and report the results to their group. All of them refused.

The longtime president of NARTH is Joseph Nicolosi, a licensed psychotherapist who teaches that any man who thinks he's gay simply "has failed to enact his masculinity." NARTH, based in Encino, Calif., is a referral service for its more than 1,000 members, who are both religious and secular ex-gay counselors (NARTH does not require members to be licensed or accredited). NARTH was founded by Charles Socarides, whose openly gay son later served in the Clinton administration as the first-ever liaison to the gay community.

One of Nicolosi's own former ex-gay patients, Daniel Gonzales, said most of his therapy sessions took place over the telephone. "Whenever I found myself attracted to a guy, I was supposed to befriend him and demystify him," said Gonzales. "It never occurred to [Nicolosi] that some of the guys I'm attracted to weren't straight." After spending a year in the $250-an-hour sessions, Gonzales didn't feel any less gay. He says he quit the therapy after realizing that "I would have to do these mental gymnastics for the rest of my life." . . .

Playing with Numbers

To back up their claims that homosexuality is purely a deviant lifestyle choice, ex-gay leaders frequently cite the Thomas Project, a four-year study of ex-gay programs, paid for by Exodus, that recruited subjects exclusively from Exodus ministries. It was conducted by Mark Yarhouse, a psychology professor at Pat Robertson's Regents University, and Stanton Jones, provost of Wheaton College, an evangelical institution in Illinois. Both are members of NARTH. The study was conducted entirely via 45-minute telephone interviews conducted annually over the course of four years. Results were published in September [2007].

Of nearly 100 people surveyed, only 11 percent reported a move towards heterosexuality. But no one in the study reports becoming fully heterosexual; according to the study's authors, even the 11 percent group "did not report themselves to be without experience of homosexual arousal, and did not report heterosexual orientation to be unequivocal and uncomplicated."

The researchers had originally hoped for 300 subjects but, according to an article in *Christianity Today*, "found many Exodus ministries mysteriously uncooperative." Over the course of the four-year study, a quarter of the participants dropped out. Their reasons for quitting were not tracked.

Nevertheless, the study was hailed by Exodus, Focus on the Family and the Southern Baptist Convention as "scientific evidence to prove what we as former homosexuals have known all along—that those who struggle with unwanted same-sex attraction can experience freedom from it."

Even more remarkably, Focus on the Family cites a 67 percent success rate. It came up with that number by counting as "successes" subjects who practice chastity or were still engaged in homosexual acts or thoughts "but expressed commitment to continue" the therapy.

The View of Mainstream Professionals

Despite the general consensus of major medical, health, and mental health professions that both heterosexuality and homosexuality are normal expressions of human sexuality, efforts to change sexual orientation through therapy have been adopted by some political and religious organizations and aggressively promoted to the public. However, such efforts have serious potential to harm young people because they present the view that the sexual orientation of lesbian, gay, and bisexual youth is a mental illness or disorder, and they often frame the inability to change one's sexual orientation as a personal and moral failure.

Because of the aggressive promotion of efforts to change sexual orientation through therapy, a number of medical, health, and mental health professional organizations have issued public statements about the dangers of this approach. The American Academy of Pediatrics, the American Counseling Association, the American Psychiatric Association, the American Psychological Association, the American School Counselor Association, the National Association of School Psychologists, and the National Association of Social Workers, together representing more than 480,000 mental health professionals, have all taken the position that homosexuality is not a mental disorder and thus is not something that needs to or can be "cured."

Just the Facts Coalition,
Sexual Orientation and Youth:
A Primer for Principals, Educators and School Personnel,
2008. www.apa.org.

Despite its rhetoric that "freedom from unwanted homosexuality is possible," Exodus officials seem quietly aware that few, if any, of the thousands of people who participate in their ministries actually change their sexual orientation. Exodus pamphlets with titles like "My Fiancé(e) is Ex-Gay: Are We Ready for Marriage?" and "Women & Ex-Gay Men: Establishing Healthy Boundaries" present ex-gay status as essentially an act of faith.

"Why do ex-gay men pursue women?" one pamphlet asks. The answers offered describe the ex-gay movement itself: "Social Expectation . . . Self-Reassurance . . . Blind Faith."

Wink and Nod

One of the first things to strike a newcomer to any Exodus conference is how much it seems to play to stereotypes of gay men. At Revolution, the name Exodus gave to its conference [in June 2007] at Concordia University in Irvine, Calif., the young men attending wore designer jeans and tight-fitting T-shirts. They had pierced ears and expensive haircuts. Burroway, the gay man who tracks the ex-gay movement for Box Turtle Bulletin, describes Exodus conferences he's attended as "one of the gayest things I have ever been to."

At the June conference in Irvine, which promised "complete, sudden, radical change," Exodus vice president Randy Thomas, the master of ceremonies, dangled his wrists as he made self-conscious jokes about how much he likes the Seattle Seahawks since Tiger Woods took them to the Stanley Cup. Announcing a free Friday afternoon for conference attendees, his voice grew high-pitched when he told the audience, "There's plenty of shopping."

In short, Exodus attendees were free to nod and wink at their gay pasts. After all, as many ex-gay leaders say, "No one chooses to struggle with same-sex attraction." But a glance at Exodus seminars reveals that the road to "healing" is paved with plenty of self-hatred.

Seminars at the Irvine conference boasted militant-sounding titles such as "A Hero's Journey: Fighting the Battle of Your Life." One of the featured speakers was Michael L.

Brown, author of *Revolution: The Call to Holy War* and a millennial Jew who once described the red T-shirts worn by his ministry students at a gay rights march counter-demonstration as "the shed blood of Christ flowing toward the gates of hell."

On Exodus' opening day, Brown's comments were no more reserved. To stand-up applause, he quoted from the Black Panthers [a militant Civil Rights group of the 1960s and 1970s] and told the thousand members of his audience that the fight against gay civil rights is a "cause worth dying for."

Before the four-day Exodus conference came to an end, Focus on the Family and Exodus spokesman Mike Haley showed a final video clip on the gargantuan multimedia screen. By that time, the audience was in a weakened emotional state. Over the past four days, they'd been repeatedly told they had failed as parents, failed as boys and girls, failed as husbands and wives, and that their failure to change may lead them to fail God as well.

The video showed a local evening news segment from a town in the Midwest. A soldier is granted an unexpected furlough from Iraq. He makes a surprise visit to his son's first-grade classroom. The boy curls up in his father's arms, crying uncontrollably. Most of the audience was soon doing the same.

"I want you all to have the strength of that little boy," said Haley.

Harm? What Harm?

The same weekend as the Exodus Revolution conference, just a mile down the road at the campus of University of California-Irvine, 100 men and women gathered for the first-ever Ex-Gay Survivor's conference, subtitled "Undoing the Damage, Affirming Our Lives Together." For some, it was a space to heal. Scott Tucker, another alumnus of LIA who is now openly gay, said that for years he faulted himself for failing to turn straight until he realized the programs had the opposite effect, isolating him in a "ghetto" of gay men trying to become straight.

For others, it was a place to challenge Exodus and turn its message of "change is possible" upside down. "Yes you can pursue change. But at what cost?" said Toscano. He and other ex-gay survivors invited Exodus president Alan Chambers and other ex-gay leaders to an off-the-record dinner. "From knowing quite a few of you personally, we know that you have a heart to help people and to serve God. You meant to bless us," read the invitation. "Too often once we leave your programs, you never hear about our lives and what happens to us."

Exodus officials declined the invitation.

Shawn O'Donnell, who spent a decade in ex-gay ministries beginning when he was 15, chalked up his experiences on a blackboard at the Ex-Gay Survivor's conference. "I see now that going through these ex-gay experiences caused harm in my life. I heard the message loud and clear that I was a horrible person. I began cutting on myself at such an early age because I just couldn't deal with the fact that I was gay," wrote O'Donnell. "I grew to hate myself and tried to take my life a few times."

O'Donnell later posted the same comments on his blog, receiving a stream of supportive comments. Exodus' Chambers, who frequently challenges the posts on ex-gay survivors' sites, wrote back: "Harm? Come on, Shawn. No one is being harmed by Exodus offering people a choice. You KNOW better."

Behind closed doors, though, Exodus' president admits to struggling with homosexuality every day of his life. "Every day, I wake up and deny what comes naturally to me," Chambers told a private audience of about 75 "strugglers" at an ex-gay conference held in Phoenix last February.

If there's any doubt where the ex-gay leaders are taking the movement, Chambers clarified it this September [2007], speaking to a Who's Who of the anti-gay Christian right at the Family Impact Summit in Brandon, Fla.

"We have to stand up against an evil agenda," Chambers told his fellow hard-liners. "It is an evil agenda and it will take anyone captive that is willing, or that is standing idly by."

Periodical Bibliography

The following articles have been selected to supplement the diverse views presented in this chapter.

Michael Abrams	"Born Gay?" *Discover*, 2007.
Adelle M. Banks	"Mohler Would Favor Altering 'Gay' Fetus," *Christian Century*, April 3, 2007.
Sharon Begley	"A New Look at Link Between Being Gay and Having Brothers," *Wall Street Journal*, (Eastern Edition), June 30, 2006.
Gary Greenberg	"Gay by Choice?" *Mother Jones*, September-October 2007.
Kelly Griffith	"Brainwashed No More," *Advocate*, August 30, 2005.
Catholic Insight	"Homosexuality Misrepresented," June 2006.
Annie Nelson	"Your Heaven, My Hell: Gays Decry 'Reorientation' Threatening Condemnation," *Columbia (MO) Daily Tribune*, November 17, 2007.
Stephen Ornes	"Do Brothers Make You Gay?" *Discover*, September 2006.
Stephen Ornes	"Gay Influence Found," *Discover*, January 2007.
Vincent Savolainen and Laurent Lehmann	"Genetics and Bisexuality." *Nature*, January 11, 2007.
Tim Stafford	"An Older, Wiser Ex-Gay Movement," *Christianity Today*, October 2007.
Elizabeth Svoboda	"All in the Family," *Science and Spirit*, September-October 2006.

CHAPTER 2

Should Gay Men and Women Serve in the Military?

Chapter Preface

According to its official Web site, the United States Army "is made up of the best-trained, most dedicated, most respected Soldiers in the world—protecting America's freedoms at home and abroad, securing our homeland, and defending democracy worldwide." For generations, American men and women have willingly placed themselves at risk for the honor of serving their country in the armed forces, and although they have not been welcomed or acknowledged, more than one million of those service members have been gay men and lesbians. But the policy of the U.S. military is that "homosexuality is incompatible with military service," and only those gay men and women who are willing to hide their sexual orientation may serve.

As a candidate for the presidency in 1992, Bill Clinton pledged to lift the longstanding ban on gay and lesbian service members, and allow all qualified people, regardless of sexual orientation, to serve. When he took office as the country's fortieth president, however, he encountered overwhelming resistance from military officers, and had to back off his pledge. Instead, a compromise measure was enacted, and given the nickname "Don't Ask, Don't Tell." Under the new policy, sexual orientation itself would not keep a man or woman from serving in the military; however, a service member would be removed from the armed forces if she or he engaged in "homosexual conduct, which is defined as a homosexual act, a statement that the member is homosexual or bisexual, or a marriage or attempted marriage to someone of the same gender." Superior officers would not ask about anyone's orientation, and so long as gay men or lesbians did not reveal that orientation they could continue to serve.

This compromise policy, in fact, pleased no one. Gay men and lesbians felt restricted, forced to hide something important to them, unable to be completely honest with their colleagues. Many heterosexual soldiers felt uncomfortable as well, worried that someone in their unit might be gay or lesbian. In some units, suspected gay men and lesbians were ostracized or bullied, and many were forced out. To respond to this treatment, the "Don't Ask, Don't Tell" policy was amended to include two new prohibitions: "Don't Pursue, Don't Harass."

When the United States went to war against Iraq in 2003, the question of who should serve in the military took on a new urgency. Suddenly there was a need, for example, for Arabic translators, and some in the military were shaken when six men fluent in Arabic were released from service because of their sexual orientation. Former chairman of the Joint Chiefs of Staff, general John Shalikashvili, who had supported the ban, wrote in 2007 that he had changed his mind, saying "Our military has been stretched thin by our deployments in the Middle East, and we must welcome the service of any American who is willing and able to do the job." But the current chairman of the Joint Chiefs, Marine general David Pace, disagreed, saying in an interview that "homosexual acts between two individuals are immoral and that we should not condone immoral acts."

The question of who should serve in the military in time of war is a complicated one. In the following chapter, the authors present a range of opinions about the potential benefits and the dangers presented by the presence of openly gay and lesbian soldiers in the armed forces.

VIEWPOINT 1

> *"The presence of open homosexuals [corrodes military excellence] by undermining the non-sexual bonding essential to unit cohesion."*

Gay Men and Women in the Military Disrupt Unit Cohesion

Mackubin Thomas Owens

In the following viewpoint, Mackubin Thomas Owens examines political dialogue about gay men and women in the military. He argues that most members of the American armed forces are opposed to open homosexual military service and concludes that permitting homosexual service would undermine essential unit cohesion. Owens is a professor of national security affairs at the Naval War College in Newport, Rhode Island, and a Vietnam War veteran who was awarded the Silver Star medal.

As you read, consider the following questions:

1. What position did John Shalikashvili hold when Bill Clinton was president, as reported in the viewpoint?

Mackubin Thomas Owens, "Ask, Tell, Whatever? Gays-in-the-Military Comes Up Again," *National Review*, vol. 59, April 16, 2007, p. 26.

2. According to the Pentagon, how many fully qualified Arabic specialists have been forced to leave the military because of "Don't Ask, Don't Tell?"
3. What is the meaning of the Greek term *philia*, as explained in the viewpoint?

For the first time since the 2000 presidential campaign, the issue of homosexuals serving openly in the military moved to center stage [again in the 2008 campaign.]. Encouraged by polls purporting to show that pubic opinion, both civilian and military, is now more receptive to the idea, Rep. Martin Meehan (D., Mass.), chairman of the relevant subcommittee, revived his 2005 bill that would repeal the Clinton-era policy of "don't ask, don't tell" (DADT). DADT prohibits military commanders from asking about a person's sexual orientation and allows homosexuals to serve if they keep their sexual orientation private and don't engage in homosexual acts. Meehan's bill would replace DADT with "a policy prohibiting discrimination on the basis of sexual orientation."

The timing of this debate is unfortunate. As David S.C. Chu, undersecretary of defense for personnel and readiness, wrote in a letter to Sen. Ron Wyden (D., Ore.), "The Global War on Terrorism is far-reaching and unrelenting." A national debate on gays in the military threatens to cause "divisiveness and turbulence across our country, [compounding] the burden of the war."

The most interesting aspect of the current debate is the change in tactics on the part of advocates of open homosexual service. In the past, they argued that this was merely the latest episode in a struggle for equal civil rights—often invoking President [Harry] Truman's postwar executive order that racially integrated the U.S. military. *Boston Globe* columnist James Carroll wrote in 2000 that "today's soldiers and sailors reluctant to serve shoulder to shoulder with homosexuals are the progeny of racist and sexist soldiers and sailors who were told to get over it or get out."

Does Exclusion Undermine Effectiveness?

But now they argue that the exclusion of homosexuals undermines military effectiveness and is at odds with public opinion. This claim is made by both liberals and conservatives. For instance, in a letter to defense secretary Robert Gates asking him to "revisit" DADT, Senator Wyden wrote that the policy "makes absolutely no sense and undermines the fight against terrorism." Wyden's office has contended that dozens of homosexual service members with critically needed skills like proficiency in Arabic have been discharged, and that enforcing the policy costs hundreds of millions of taxpayer dollars.

Wyden has always opposed the exclusion of open homosexuals, but even some who once favored the exclusion are making the same argument. In January [2007], retired Army general John Shalikashvili, chairman of the Joint Chiefs of Staff under President [Bill] Clinton, wrote in the *New York Times* that he had reconsidered his position and concluded that the current policy should be reversed. He based his change of heart on his belief that the U.S. military has been "stretched thin," and that public sentiment has shifted in recent years. Former Republican senator Alan Simpson has made essentially the same arguments in a *Washington Post* op-ed.

There are several problems with these arguments. First, the numbers used by opponents of DADT to support their position are questionable. For example, the main evidence for the contention that there is greater public acceptance of open homosexual service, both within and outside of the military, is a Zogby International poll published in December 2006. But as Elaine Donnelly's Center for Military Readiness has pointed out, Zogby chose to highlight the response to an irrelevant question: "Are you comfortable interacting with gay people?" Seventy-three percent of respondents replied that they were.

But in response to the central question ("Do you agree or disagree with allowing gays and lesbians to serve openly in the military?"), only 26 percent agreed, while 37 percent disagreed and 32 percent were neutral. That is hardly indicative of overwhelming public support for open homosexual service.

Service Members Oppose Homosexual Service

The numbers purporting to show that military members favor open homosexual service are fishy as well. The Zogby news release stated that the poll was designed in conjunction with the Michael D. Palm Center (formerly the Center for the Study of Sexual Minorities in the Military), an advocacy group that has long pushed for open homosexual service. This fact may or not have an impact on the credibility of the poll. But the polling sample does: It claims to be based on a sample of 545 people "who have served in Iraq and Afghanistan (or in combat support roles directly supporting those operations), from a purchased list of U.S. military personnel." But, as Donnelly observes, the U.S. military does not sell or provide access to personnel lists.

The Zogby figures are further called into question by a January 2007 *Military Times* survey of active-duty subscribers, which found that while 30 percent thought that open homosexuals ought to be permitted to serve, 59 percent did not, and 10 percent had no opinion. The 59 percent opposed to open homosexual service was identical to that revealed by a January 2006 survey conducted by the same paper.

Then there is the question of the effect of DADT on the retention of crucial personnel, such as Arabic linguists. Advocates of open homosexual service have made a big deal of this, claiming, for instance, that fifty-four Arab linguists have been separated from the military because they were homosexual. But the Pentagon has argued that most of those who are counted among the fifty-four had not achieved linguistic

Military Opposition to Homosexual Servicemembers

In 2007, active duty military subscribers to the Military Times newspapers were asked, "Do you think openly homosexual people should be allowed to serve in the military?"

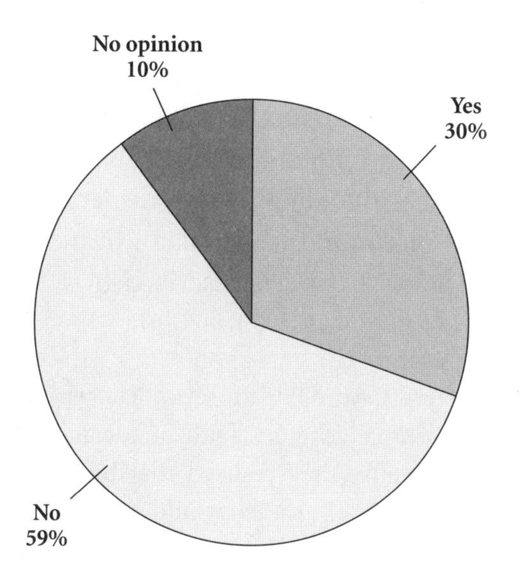

TAKEN FROM: *Army Times*, Jan. 8, 2007.

proficiency, and that over a decade only nine qualified Arabic specialists have been separated because of the law.

But let's address the broadest question: Why prohibit open homosexual service at all? Congress provided the answer in 1993, when it passed the current law: "Homosexuality is incompatible with military service and presents a risk to the morale, good order and discipline, and unit cohesion that underpin military effectiveness."

An important element of war is "friction" which [Prussian military thinker Carl von] Clausewitz described as "the only concept that more or less corresponds to the factors that distinguish real war from war on paper." Clausewitz's friction describes the cumulative effect of the small, often unnoticeable events that are amplified in war, producing unanticipated macro-effects. Military effectiveness aims at reducing the impact of friction and other obstacles to success on the battlefield.

The Concept of Philia

Most research has shown unit cohesion is critical to military effectiveness and battlefield success. The key to cohesion is what the Greeks called *philia*—friendship, comradeship, or brotherly love. Philia is the bond among disparate individuals who have nothing in common but facing death and misery together. Its importance has been described by J. Glenn Gray in *The Warriors: Reflections on Men in Battle*:

> Numberless soldiers have died, more or less willingly, not for country or honor or religious faith or for any other abstract good, but because they realized that by fleeing their posts and rescuing themselves, they would expose their companions to greater danger. Such loyalty to the group is the essence of fighting morale. The commander who can preserve and strengthen it knows that all other physical and psychological factors are little in comparison. The feeling of loyalty, it is clear, is the result, not the cause, of comradeship. Comrades are loyal to each other spontaneously and without any need for reasons.

The presence of open homosexuals (and women) in the close confines of ships or military units opens the possibility that eros will be unleashed into an environment based on philia, creating friction and corroding the very source of military excellence itself. It does so by undermining the nonsexual bonding essential to unit cohesion as described by Gray. Unlike philia, eros is sexual and therefore individual and exclusive. Eros manifests itself as sexual competition, protectiveness, and favoritism, all of which undermine order, discipline, and morale. These are issues of life and death, and help to explain why open homosexuality and homosexual behavior traditionally have been considered incompatible with military service.

But can't these problems be solved by enforcing regulations against fraternization and sexual relations among service members? There are indeed such regulations on the books, but they cannot always be enforced. And when they are not, the consequences extend far beyond the individuals involved. Over the past two decades I have seen the poisonous effects that personal relationships gone wrong can have in an academic setting. But no one died. In combat, the consequences could well be lethal.

Finally, some advocates of open homosexual service—e.g., Senator Simpson—observe that it has not had an adverse effect on other militaries in the world. But where it matters most—in combat units—these other militaries follow pretty much the same policy as the United States.

In the end, it is up to Congress to decide whether to change the law. As Prof. Charles Moskos of Northwestern University, dean of American military sociologists and the primary architect of the DADT policy, pointed out several years ago in the *Wall Street Journal*, there are foolish reasons for excluding homosexuals from the armed forces, but that does not mean we should ignore the good ones. Chief among the good reasons remains military effectiveness.

VIEWPOINT 2

"Twenty-four countries have lifted their bans on homosexual service members without undermining cohesion."

Gay Men and Women in the Military Do Not Disrupt Unit Cohesion

Gregory M. Herek and Aaron Belkin

In the following viewpoint, Gregory Herek and Aaron Belkin review the evidence that gay men and women should be banned from military service because their presence adversely affects unit cohesion. They argue that units actually perform well together—regardless of the sexual orientation of their members—if they share the same goals. Herek is a professor of psychology at the University of California at Davis and a past chairperson of the American Psychological Association Committee on Lesbian and Gay Concerns. Belkin is a professor of political science at the University of California at Berkeley, specializing in civil-military relations and security studies, with a focus on sexuality and the military.

Gregory M. Herek and Aaron Belkin, *Military Life: The Psychology of Serving in Peace and Combat: Volume 4: Military Culture*. Westport, CT: Praeger Security International, 2005.

As you read, consider the following questions:

1. As the viewpoint explains, what is the difference between "social cohesion" and "task cohesion?"
2. Why can too much social cohesion harm a unit's effectiveness, according to a study by Robert J. MacCoun?
3. When did Canada end its ban on gay and lesbian service members, according to the viewpoint?

Over the past fifty years, military and political officials have articulated many different rationales for excluding gay and lesbian service members. At various times, they have argued that gay men and lesbians are mentally and physically unfit for military service, pose security risks, engage in sexual misconduct more often than their heterosexual counterparts, threaten unit cohesion, and violate the privacy of heterosexual service members.

Some of these rationales are no longer credible to most military officials and scholars. Since the 1980s, a consensus has emerged among policy makers that homosexual men and women are fully capable of serving in the military and that many have done so despite policies that officially excluded them. During House Budget Committee hearings in 1992, for example, General Colin Powell, then-chairman of the Joint Chiefs of Staff, stated that the reason for keeping lesbians and gay men out of the military "is not an argument of performance on the part of homosexuals who might be in uniform, and it is not saying they are not good enough." He further characterized individuals "who favor a homosexual lifestyle" as "proud, brave, loyal, good Americans." In 1991 testimony before the same House committee, then-Secretary of Defense Dick Cheney referred to the policy of the time concerning gay people and security clearances as "an old chestnut."

What remains contested is whether the presence of acknowledged gay men and lesbians in the military would adversely affect heterosexual service members because of the latter's discomfort with homosexuality and gay people. Thus, the unit cohesion and privacy rationales now dominate the discussion of whether gay men and lesbians could serve openly in the U.S. military without compromising military effectiveness.

Unit Cohesion

The unit cohesion rationale is the official justification for the current DADT ["Don't Ask, Don't Tell"] law and policies that regulate gay and lesbian service members, and it is premised on the idea that the military must exclude known gay and lesbian service members if it is to maintain morale, good order, and discipline—qualities associated with unit cohesion. According to this perspective, heterosexual service members dislike gay men and lesbians to such an extent that they would be unable to work with them and trust them with their lives, thereby destroying the bonds necessary for units to function effectively. This rationale emerged in the policies articulated by the military in 1975 and 1981 in response to court decisions.

The research literature on cohesion is vast, and the construct has been defined, described, and measured in numerous ways, often reflecting prevailing societal conditions and the values and interests of the scholars conducting the research. Early academic research on cohesion tended to define it as a property of the group that resulted from positive social relationships among group members. The military has often related cohesion to combat, emphasizing the loyalty that service members feel toward each other, the group, and their leaders as they accomplish dangerous and life-threatening missions. [A 2003 study,] for example, argued that U.S. soldiers in Operation Iraqi Freedom developed trusting relationships, or cohesion, by withstanding hardship and enduring austere conditions together, and that these emotional bonds played a primary role in motivating them to fight.

Statement of Twenty-eight Generals and Admirals:

We respectfully urge Congress to repeal the "don't ask, don't tell" policy. Those of us signing this letter have dedicated our lives to defending the rights of our citizens to believe whatever they wish. As General Colin Powell, former chairman of the Joint Chiefs said when the "don't ask, don't tell" policy was enacted, it is not the place of the military or those in senior leadership to make moral judgments.

Scholarly data shows there are approximately one million gay and lesbian veterans in the United States today, as well as 65,000 gays and lesbians currently serving in our armed forces. They have served our nation honorably.

We support the recent comments of another former chairman of the Joint Chiefs, General John Shalikashvili, who has concluded that repealing the "don't ask, don't tell" policy would not harm, and would indeed help, our armed forces. As is the case in Britain, Israel, and other nations which allow gays and lesbians to serve openly, our service members are professionals who are able to work together effectively despite differences in race, gender, religion, and sexuality. Such collaboration reflects the strength and the best traditions of our democracy.

Statement to Congress, November 30, 2007. www.palmcenter.org.

Cohesion is not a unitary construct and multiple dimensions of cohesion have been discussed in the research literature. Perhaps the most common distinction made by behavioral scientists is between *social cohesion* (the nature and quality of the emotional bonds of friendship, liking, caring, and closeness among group members) and *task cohesion* (members' shared commitment to achieving a goal that requires the collective efforts of the group). A group displays high social cohesion to the extent that its members like each other, prefer to spend their social time together, enjoy each other's company, and feel emotionally close to one another. A group with high task cohesion is composed of members who share a common goal and who are motivated to coordinate their efforts to achieve that goal as a team.

The Debate over Cohesion

The debate about the correlation between group cohesion and performance continues. For example, based on interviews with approximately forty service members who reported on their own motivations for fighting during combat in Iraq, [Leonard] Wong et al. argued that social cohesion is an important determinant of unit performance. While their approach may have yielded an accurate impression of respondents' perceptions, however, it is not methodologically adequate for determining whether combat effectiveness actually resulted from social cohesion or another source for which they failed to control, in particular task cohesion.

Indeed, most scholars agree that social cohesion cannot be seen as the primary cause for high levels of military performance. Rather, task cohesion seems to be more important. Successfully accomplishing a challenging task as a group, combined with familiarity but not social similarity, increases small-unit cohesion. Effective leadership at the unit level is also a key element for creating cohesion. After reviewing military and civilian studies of cohesion and performance, [Robert J.] MacCoun concluded that task cohesion—not social cohesion or group pride—drives group performance. He pointed out that when social cohesion is too high, deleterious consequences can result, including excessive socializing, groupthink (the failure of a highly cohesive group to engage in effective decision-making processes), insubordination, and mutiny. MacCoun concluded that the impact—if any—of a new sexual orientation policy would be on social cohesion. Because coworkers can perform effectively as a team without necessarily liking each other, he argued, such a reduction in cohesion would be unlikely to reduce the military's ability to complete its mission successfully.

Thus, notwithstanding a few studies such as that by Wong et al., the literature raises serious questions about the validity of the unit cohesion rationale. Because unit cohesion is more influenced by the successful completion of tasks and sharing of common goals than by social similarity, the presence of known gay or lesbian service members should have little negative impact so long as they share the same goals as their colleagues.

Discretion Is the Norm

Another problem with the unit cohesion rationale is that it fails to acknowledge that most gay and lesbian service members exercise considerable discretion in revealing their homosexuality to others and are likely to continue doing so even if DADT is eliminated. Research on foreign militaries suggests that when bans on homosexual service members are lifted, relatively few gay and lesbian personnel disclose their sexual orientation. Although the Canadian military estimated that 3.5 percent of its personnel were gay or lesbian, for example, the Department of National Defense received only seventeen claims for medical, dental, and relocation benefits for same-sex partners in 1998, six years after Canada lifted its ban. This suggests that service members were reluctant to identify themselves by requesting benefits. Similarly, only thirty-three soldiers identified themselves openly as gay or lesbian to a research team three years after Australia lifted its ban, although it is reasonable to assume that the actual number of gay service members was considerably larger. If most gay and lesbian service members do not reveal their sexual orientation, it seems unlikely that their homosexuality would pose a serious threat to the effective operation of their unit.

Finally, even when a unit includes openly gay and lesbian personnel, experience does not indicate that cohesion suffers as a consequence. [Historian Allan] Bérubé provided extensive evidence [in 1990] that many lesbians and gay men served more or less openly in the U.S. military during World War II. Their sexual orientation was known to many of their heterosexual comrades, and they served effectively in combat with the respect and admiration of those comrades. More recently, the literature includes case studies of individuals such as Margarethe Cammermeyer and Perry Watkins who served openly [in the Vietnam War] without undermining their units' cohesion. More generally, in countries that have lifted gay bans, there have been no reports that the small number of gay and lesbian personnel who came out compromised military performance, readiness, or unit cohesion in any way. The fact that twenty-four countries have lifted their bans on homosexual service members without undermining cohesion suggests that the U.S. military's rationale may not reflect military necessity. Indeed, the U.S. military itself has refrained from enforcing the ban when personnel were needed for combat operations, the time when cohesion matters most to the military mission. As noted above, many homosexual recruits were accepted and retained for service during World War II when all available personnel were needed. And during the first Gulf War, the ban was effectively suspended via stop-loss order without any apparent impact on cohesion or readiness.

Viewpoint 3

"Open homosexuality in the ranks will negatively impact the propensity for many young people to enlist."

The Military Is Better Off Without Gay Men and Women

Robert Maginnis

In the following viewpoint, Robert Maginnis considers arguments for and against banning gay men and women from serving in the military and concludes that the only issue is whether an individual's service truly aids the military. He argues that military service is not a right, and the demands of cohesion and readiness dictate that gay men and women should not serve. He further contends that lifting the ban on gay men and women serving in the military would lead conservatives to avoid enlisting, thus reducing the size and strength of our force. Maginnis is a retired army lieutenant colonel, a senior strategist with the U.S. Army, and a national security and foreign affairs analyst.

As you read, consider the following questions:

1. Why did President Bill Clinton not keep his campaign promise to allow gay men and women to serve in the military, according to the viewpoint?

Robert Maginnis, "Gays in the Military Debate—Deja vu 1993?" www.humanevents.com., October 4, 2007. Reproduced by permission.

2. What are three characteristics and behaviors that have led to service personnel being dismissed from the military, as reported in the viewpoint?
3. According to the author, what qualities do Americans who volunteer to serve in the armed forces share?

[In September 2007] Marine General Peter Pace, the outgoing chairman of the Joint Chiefs of Staff, restated his support for the military's homosexual ban, a view shared by all Republican presidential candidates. [Former] Democratic Senator Tom Harkin (Iowa) said Pace's "immoral" label for homosexuality was "hurtful" and "demoralizing," a position embraced by Democratic presidential candidates. Is it déjà vu 1993?

In 1992, presidential candidate Bill Clinton pledged to lift the ban but he ran into a firestorm of opposition when he took office. After a contentious six month national debate, Congress sent Clinton a strict exclusion statute (10 USC § 654) which he signed. However, the Pentagon drew up contrary implementing regulations known as "don't ask, don't tell" (DADT). The law excludes homosexuals from the military but the Clinton-era regulations say soldiers need not declare their sexual orientation and the military can't ask about it.

Once again, a political fight is brewing over the ban on gays serving openly. Democratic presidential candidate Senator Hillary Clinton describes her husband's DADT compromise as a "transition policy" that is no longer "the best way to proceed." She argues that the military should regulate behavior, not orientation. Apparently the senator fails to understand that those with a homosexual orientation tend to behave consistent with it, which is a problem for the military. Clinton's fellow Democratic presidential candidates share her DADT view.

A Long-Standing Tradition

On March 14, 1778, General George Washington issued a General Order at Valley Forge, removing a soldier from the armed forces for homosexual behavior:

> Head Quarters, V. Forge, Saturday, March 14, 1778: At a General Court Martial whereof Colo. Tupper was President (10th March 1778) Lieutt. Enslin of Colo. Malcom's Regiment tried for attempting to commit *sodomy*, with John Monhort a soldier; Secondly, For Perjury in swearing to false Accounts, found guilty of the charges exhibited against him, being breaches of 5th. Article 18th. Section of the Articles of War and do sentence him to be dismiss'd the service with Infamy. His Excellency the Commander in Chief approves the sentence and with Abhorrence and Detestation of such Infamous Crimes orders Lieutt. Enslin to be drummed out of Camp tomorrow morning by all the Drummers and Fifers in the Army never to return; The Drummers and Fifers to attend on the Grand Parade at Guard mounting for that Purpose. [emphasis in the original].

George Washington, The Writings of George Washington, *ed. John C. Fitzpatrick. Washington, D.C.: U.S. Government Printing Office, 1934. pp.83–84.*

Republicans contend that the current policy is working. Rudolph Giuliani, [for a time] the presidential front runner, argues that "at a time of war, you don't make fundamental changes like this." His peers support that position.

The policy question should be: Does the homosexual ban satisfy military necessity? The 1993 Congress thought it did and, so far, six appellate courts have agreed. The would-be candidates of both parties should explain how their homosexual policy position will sustain combat effectiveness, which requires both unit cohesion and readiness.

No Right to Serve

The 1993 ban is premised on the fact that there is no constitutional right to serve. Thus, Congress may decide who should or should not serve. For [at least] 231 years, the U.S. military has discriminated among potential recruits based on a variety of characteristics and behaviors, with the intent of forming the best possible force. That's why, according to the General Accountability Office, the Pentagon discharged 59,098 service personnel for drug offenses, 26,513 for weight standards and 9,501 for homosexuality between 1993 and 2004.

Under American civilian law, few employers can fire someone for being overweight. In civilian life, no one would lump drug use, obesity and homosexuality in the same category. But in the military, they are all factors that affect the bottom line: unit cohesion and combat effectiveness. So they have to be dealt with in similar ways.

Military service requires a unique blend of skills, ethics, culture, and bonding to ensure an effective fighting force. Soldiers must be constantly available for worldwide deployment to a combat environment. There is often no escape from this structured environment for weeks and sometimes months on end. Active service places demands and constraints upon its soldiers, not the least of which are bathing and sleeping in close quarters.

The uniqueness of military life knows few bounds. It begins on the first day of boot camp and continues until the soldier is discharged. Their conduct is subject to the Uniform Code of Military Justice at all times—on and off base and on and off duty.

Cohesion Is Essential

Combat effectiveness grows in this unique medium by building ready and cohesive units. These units are built and sustained through constant and close associations over long periods. Unquestioned trust and confidence are essential to them. They are sustained on a diet of fairness and absence of favoritism.

Cohesion is the indispensable glue that holds units together. It's the single most important factor in a unit's ability to succeed on the battlefield. In 1993, chairman of the Joint Chiefs of Staff General Colin Powell told Congress:

> "To win wars, we create cohesive teams of warriors who will bond so tightly that they are prepared to go into battle and give their lives if necessary for the accomplishment of the mission. . . . We cannot allow anything to happen which would disrupt that feeling of cohesion within the force."

Sexual tensions and sex-based favoritism in intimate settings destroy cohesion, whether they involve opposite- or same-sex attraction. If we respect women's need for privacy from men, then we ought to respect the same need on the part of heterosexuals with regard to homosexuals. Protecting privacy in a military with open homosexuality would necessitate recognizing essentially four sexes and would severely disrupt units.

The military has successfully put soldiers from very diverse backgrounds into long term close quarters situations. Behavior, especially sexual behavior that deviates from the norm, undercuts the cohesion of the group. Therefore, most military professionals consider such behavior detrimental to the development and maintenance of cohesive units.

Open Homosexuality Will Erode Readiness

The other component of combat effectiveness is readiness, medical and personnel. In 1993, the Army's surgeon general conceded that the homosexual lifestyle is unhealthy. A Navy study has found that HIV infections within the force have declined since passage of the 1993 ban. This has likely saved the taxpayer medical costs. It is significant that HIV positive service members, although retained in the military, may not be deployed overseas or on ships.

Recruitment of a quality volunteer force is a readiness challenge especially in wartime. Open homosexuality in the ranks will negatively impact the propensity for many young people to enlist due to the influence of parents, teachers and pastors. Americans most likely to serve voluntarily tend to be conservative and religious, the demographic least likely to embrace homosexuality.

Retention of the serving force could also be affected by lifting the ban. Military personnel tend to be conservative and self-identify with one of 104 faith groups that share General Pace's view that homosexual behavior is "counter to God's law."

However unequal and discriminatory the military's homosexual ban may seem, it is necessary to protect the services' combat effectiveness which is the product of unit cohesion and readiness.

In the end, the burden of proof that lifting the ban would do no harm rests with those who would change the policy. So far, the [2008] Democrat presidential candidates and the radical homosexual community have offered no credible proof to that effect.

VIEWPOINT 4

> *"Taxpayers have spent a quarter of a billion dollars training replacements for gay service members kicked out since 'Don't ask, don't tell' was first implemented."*

Gay Men and Women Make Important Contributions to Our Military Effort

C. Dixon Osburn

In the following viewpoint, C. Dixon Osburn discusses the consequences of the U.S. military's current "Don't ask, don't tell policy," under which the Pentagon discharges well over a thousand people every year for being gay, lesbian, or bisexual. Osburn contends that we need the talents of these men and women, and that we spend a considerable amount of money training replacements when studies have shown gay men and women perform just as well as their straight counterparts and do not undermine military cohesion. The military, the author contends, is unnecessarily weakening itself by banning gay men and women from serving. C. Dixon Osburn is executive director and cofounder of the Servicemembers Legal Defense Network in Washington, DC.

C. Dixon Osburn, "Colleges Cave to Pentagon Threat," *The Gay & Lesbian Review Worldwide*, March-April 2003. Reproduced by permission.

As you read, consider the following questions:

1. According to the author, how many linguists have been discharged from the military because of their sexual orientation?
2. What percent of service members had heard anti-gay epithets, according to the viewpoint?
3. Why did Harvard University, along with many others, create an exception in its nondiscrimination policy for the armed forces, as cited by Osburn?

Under the U.S. military's current "Don't ask, don't tell" policy, the Pentagon discharges well over a thousand people every year for being gay, lesbian, or bisexual. This policy is just the latest incarnation of an ongoing witch hunt that has been in operation since the Second World War.

The Pentagon fires three to four people every day for being gay—over 1,000 people each year. More than 115,000 gay and lesbian service members have been discharged since the War. Service members have had nooses placed on their necks, been beaten with pillow sacks filled with bars of soap, raped, murdered, discharged—all for being, or being perceived as, lesbian, gay or bisexual. They have had their diaries seized for information about their private lives, and been dragged away in handcuffs on suspicion of being gay.

We Need the Talents of Soldiers Discharged for Their Sexuality

No American is left untouched by this policy. As a nation, we lose the talents and skills of those critical for our national security. The Army recently fired seven Arabic linguists for being gay despite a severe shortage of linguists in our fight against terrorism. Taxpayers have spent a quarter of a billion dollars training replacements for gay servicemembers kicked out since "Don't ask, don't tell" was first implemented. Gay Americans not in the military suffer as judges, CEOs, and politicians invoke "Don't ask, don't tell" as justification for anti-gay rights initiatives, the Boy Scouts' exclusionary policies, and denial of civilian job rights.

Some Americans who serve our country proudly, however, are especially at risk.

Women are discharged at a rate twice their presence in the armed forces. In 2001, 30 percent of those discharged under "Don't ask, don't tell" were women, though women comprised only 14 percent of the active duty force. In the Air Force, where women comprise 19 percent of the active duty force, 43 percent of those discharged were women. African American women are especially targeted. Many female service-members are accused of being lesbians for retaliatory reasons—because they report sexual harassment or refuse the sexual advances of male colleagues. Other women are accused of being lesbians simply because they serve in non-traditional job fields.

Younger men and women are also disproportionately impacted by the Pentagon's gay ban. The military is the largest employer of men and women in the 18–25 age bracket. While young adults comprise approximately 42 percent of the armed forces, 90 percent of Marine Corps and Navy discharges in 2001, and 79 percent of the Coast Guard's gay discharges, were young adults.

Low-income Americans are also targeted. The vast majority of those discharged under "Don't ask, don't tell" earn only $12,000 to $20,000 annually. Many Americans join the military to escape poverty or overcome the limited opportunities in their small towns, only to have their one economic opportunity cut short.

Gay Soldiers Endure Harassment

Anti-gay harassment is common in the armed forces. A recent Department of Defense survey reported that 80 percent of service members had heard anti-gay epithets. The same survey found that 37 percent had witnessed or experienced incidents of anti-gay harassment, 9 percent reported witnessing threats, and 5 percent reported witnessing or experiencing physical assaults. The report further noted that 85 percent of those surveyed said their commands tolerate anti-gay harassment.

"Don't ask, don't tell" forces service members to hide, lie and evade twenty-four hours a day, seven days a week. Military personnel cannot reveal their sexual orientation to anyone—not to a parent, a friend, a psychotherapist, or a colleague—without the risk of losing his or her job, scholarships, training, and other opportunities. Imagine being forced to live a lie as your friends and colleagues ask, "Why aren't you married?" "Who was that on the phone?" "Who did you go on vacation with?" or "Who's this in the photo?" For heterosexual service members, the answers come easily. For lesbian, gay, and bisexual service members, they come with a heavy pair of alternatives: the sacrifice of personal honor and integrity or the end of a career.

The implications of federally sanctioned discrimination are devastating and far-reaching. The military is the largest employer in the United States, with 2.5 million service members on active duty and in the Reserves. It has the only law that mandates firing someone because of his or her sexual orientation. As lesbian, gay, and bisexual Americans are fired from the services, the federal government sends a clear message that gay Americans are second-class citizens, deserving of discrimination and harassment, both within and outside of the military. This blatant discrimination must not stand. And law schools must do what they can to oppose it.

Law Schools Forced to Pick a Side

Law schools across the country, including Harvard, are currently facing a major test of their moral mettle. Will they support anti-gay harassment and discrimination, or not? At issue for Harvard Law School is whether it should allow military recruiters and ROTC programs on campus, even if doing so

One Sailor's Story

An intelligence analyst, [one] sailor joined the Navy six years ago [in 2001] to see the world and to contribute to something bigger than himself, and he . . . reenlisted for another four years of service.

"Plain and simple, we, as gay Americans, just want to serve, defend, and be a part of something that's been around longer than all of us and will be around for many years after us," he writes of his desire to be in the military. But he is obviously frustrated by "don't ask, don't tell"—an outdated and discriminatory policy if ever there were one.

"Here's some irony," he writes in an e-mail. "As I sit here and type this message, I am also working on a classified briefing concerning terrorists who we are helping to track down. How funny is it that I'm here trying to help inform people of bad guys who are trying to kill innocents of their own country as well as many Americans, but if I was found out to be gay I'd be yanked out of here so fast?" Indeed. Under "don't ask, don't tell," *he'd* be the bad guy.

Marc Haeringer, "Coming Out In the Line of Fire," Advocate, *July 3, 2007.*

would violate its long-standing policy of requiring potential employers to sign a statement that they will not discriminate against lesbians, gays, and bisexuals. The U.S. military has refused to comply with university policy because the federal statute known as "Don't ask, don't tell" specifically authorizes anti-gay discrimination.

Until recently, Harvard and many other law schools had banned military recruiters from campus. The Pentagon got around the blockade through Congress, which passed the Solomon Amendment, a law that threatens to cut off all federal funding to universities that do not permit military recruiters on campus. Faced with the threat of losing $325 million in federal funding, Harvard, like many other universities, caved, creating an exception in its non-discrimination policy for the armed forces.

There is a growing and justifiable sense of outrage among students, faculty, and alumni/[various] who believe that the principle of non-discrimination should not be so cavalierly tossed aside when it comes to the rights of lesbians, gays, and bisexuals. Would Harvard have so easily caved had the military adopted a formal policy of excluding Jews or African-Americans? In the 1980s, students, faculty, and alumni/[various] came together to force their universities to divest funds from South Africa in protest of a government that supported the institutionalized racism of apartheid. Today, we should come together again to demand that the university not support a government that institutionalizes anti-gay discrimination and harassment under "Don't ask, don't tell."

It's important also to note what this debate is not about. Allowing military recruiters and ROTC on campus is not about access or recruiting. Recruitment offices are in virtually every corner of our nation. The Internet has opened up new possibilities for enlistment. Americans who want to serve can and should. The services have all met their recruiting goals for 2002. And the debate is not about patriotism in the wake of 9/11. Lesbians, gays, and bisexuals are brave, patriotic Americans who put their lives on the line for our country every day in defense of our liberties and freedoms even while denied their own at home.

A Soldier's Performance Is Not Undermined by His or Her Sexuality

Nor is this a debate about military readiness. Bigotry undermines military readiness. "Don't ask, don't tell" harms national security as we lose critical personnel, and commanders focus on people's bedroom behavior rather than their job performance. Twenty-four nations have dropped their ban on gays and lesbians in the military—including such battle-tested forces as those of Great Britain and Israel—and all report that lifting their bans has been a non-event. Every credible military study, including a $1.3 million Rand study commissioned by the Pentagon, has concluded that lifting the militia's gay ban would work fine.

What this debate is about is whether universities can be bribed into ignoring their policies of non-discrimination when it applies to lesbians, gays, and bisexuals. It's about whether the armed forces will play by the same rules as all other potential employers who come to campuses to recruit students. Many university presidents have said that permitting military recruiters on campus in no way signals a lessening of commitment to equality. That is disingenuous at best. Harvard's president, Larry Summers, has appropriately condemned Harvard's witch hunt of gay students in the 1920s that has recently come to light. But is Harvard so much better when it accepts hundreds of millions of dollars from an institution that witch hunts lesbian, gay, and bisexual Americans today?

What should Harvard Law School and its sister institutions do? The most principled stand would be to "divest," to be willing to forego the Pentagon's research grants. But if universities banded together, the military would have to back down and the Solomon Amendment would have no teeth. For the armed forces don't want to lose the talents and skills of the university researchers any more than the universities want to lose the federal funding. (Some have suggested filing a lawsuit, but the likelihood of success is minimal and will not cure the underlying discrimination.)

Investing in Equality

But if Harvard is unwilling to take the most principled stand, it should invest in equality an amount equal to what it is receiving to deny equality. It should invest in lesbian, gay, and bisexual equality in an amount equal to at least 1 percent of the funds it would have lost had it stood for non-discrimination. If Harvard gains $325 million by forcing the law school to discriminate, it should invest $3.25 million in an effort to end discrimination and harassment based on sexual orientation in the military. Underwriting a conference, hosting guest speakers, endowing an academic studies program or fellowships would all be good starts, but not sufficient given the magnitude of discrimination being endorsed. Harvard should invest in national, state, and local organizations that are fighting anti-gay discrimination and harassment on the front lines, and—along with its sister institutions—should hire a team of lobbyists, as it does on other matters of importance to it, to oppose the Solomon Amendment and "Don't ask, don't tell."

Such an investment would indicate a return to Harvard's strong commitment to non-discrimination for every patriotic American. And patriotism is, after all, about honoring the nation's core values of freedom and equality for all. The federal government should not be exempt from such noble ideals, and respected institutions such as Harvard should play a lead role in changing the military's ways.

VIEWPOINT 5

"Congress ably debated the issue . . . and reached a consensus reconciling personal freedoms with the most critical of military requirements."

The "Don't Ask, Don't Tell" Policy Is Effective and Necessary

John McCain

The following viewpoint was originally written as a letter from Republican Senator John McCain of Arizona to the Servicemembers Legal Defense Network, a group that advocates for the rights of gay men and women to serve in the United States Armed Forces. McCain explains that the "Don't Ask, Don't Tell" policy was drafted after serious consideration, and that it has the support of Congress, the military, and the courts. He argues that the policy serves the needs of the military, which must outweigh the interests of a small group of individuals. McCain is a combat veteran and a member of the Senate Armed Services Committee, and he ran for president of the United States in 2000 and 2008.

As you read, consider the following questions:

1. As the author relates it, which branch of the military did he serve in?

John McCain, "Letter to C. Dixon Osburn, Servicemembers Legal Defense Network," April 16, 2007. www.sldn.org.

2. When was the policy known as "Don't Ask, Don't Tell" debated and developed in the Senate, according to the viewpoint?
3. According to the viewpoint's quotation from Colin Powell, how is incorporating gay men and women into a military unit different from incorporating members of other groups?

I must state at the outset that I do not believe the government should unnecessarily interfere in the private lives of its citizens. That said, I do believe that any policy requiring the Armed Services to accommodate a particular lifestyle of whatever description is misguided.

I have grappled with the issue of homosexuals in the military as both a career Navy officer and a member of the Senate Armed Services Committee. Although I do not expect the controversy surrounding gay and lesbian servicemembers to recede in the foreseeable future, I believe Congress ably debated the issue in 1993 and reached a consensus reconciling personal freedoms with the most critical of military requirements—maintaining the high standards of morale, good order and discipline, and unit cohesion that form the core of military capability.

Following some of the most extensive hearings I have witnessed during all my years in Congress, the Senate Armed Services and House National Security Committees developed legislation in 1993 to effectively resolve the divisive debate over the role of homosexual servicemembers in our armed forces. This legislation, incorporated into the Fiscal Year 1994 National Defense Authorization Act, institutionalized the current policy that is colloquially referred to as "don't ask, don't tell."

Balancing Rights and Responsibilities

The legislation, which I supported, does not require the military to ask recruits whether they are homosexual, but makes their behavior the basis for determining their sexual orienta-

"Don't Ask, Don't Tell"

The policy prohibiting homosexuals and bisexuals from serving in the U.S. Armed Forces, often called "Don't Ask, Don't Tell," is actually Title 10, section 654, "Policy Concerning Homosexuality in the Armed Forces" of the U.S. Code. Part (a) of the policy lists 15 "findings" made by Congress, including the following:

> (12) The worldwide deployment of United States military forces, the international responsibilities of the United States, and the potential for involvement of the armed forces in actual combat routinely make it necessary for members of the armed forces involuntarily to accept living conditions and working conditions that are often spartan, primitive, and characterized by forced intimacy with little or no privacy.
>
> (13) The prohibition against homosexual conduct is a longstanding element of military law that continues to be necessary in the unique circumstances of military service.
>
> (14) The armed forces must maintain personnel policies that exclude persons whose presence in the armed forces would create an unacceptable risk to the armed forces' high standards of morale, good order and discipline, and unit cohesion that are the essence of military capability.
>
> (15) The presence in the armed forces of persons who demonstrate a propensity or intent to engage in homosexual acts would create an unacceptable risk to the high standards of morale, good order and discipline, and unit cohesion that are the essence of military capability.

U.S. Code, Title 10, Section 654.

tion. Thus, the Department of Defense does not ask questions exploring the sexual orientation of prospective servicemembers, and individuals are required to keep their homosexuality to themselves. However, the legislation unambiguously maintains that open homosexuality within the military services presents an intolerable risk to morale, cohesion, and discipline.

This policy is supported by the Congress and the Joint Chiefs of Staff. It has also been upheld by the Supreme Court, which has ruled that the military may constitutionally discharge a servicemember for overt homosexual behavior.

As General Colin Powell stated when he served as chairman of the Joint Chiefs of Staff, "We have successfully mixed rich and poor, black and white, male and female, but open homosexuality in [military] units is not just the acceptance of benign characteristics such as color or gender or background. . . . The presence of open homosexuality would have an unacceptable, detrimental, and disruptive impact on the cohesion, morale, and esprit of the armed forces."

I believe polarization of personnel and breakdown of unit effectiveness is too high a price to pay for well-intentioned but misguided efforts to elevate the interests of a minority of homosexual servicemembers above those of their units. Most importantly, the national security of the United States, not to mention the lives of our men and women in uniform, are put at grave risk by policies detrimental to the good order and discipline which so distinguish America's Armed Services. For these reasons, which have nothing to do with my personal judgments about homosexual behavior, I remain opposed to the open expression of homosexuality in the U.S. military.

Viewpoint

"In the interest of national security, repealing the ban on openly gay service members needs to happen sooner rather than later."

The "Don't Ask, Don't Tell" Policy Is Not Effective or Necessary

Laura Kiritsy

In the following viewpoint, Laura Kiritsy argues that the military's "Don't Ask, Don't Tell" policy keeps able men and women from contributing important skills, while less-qualified people are allowed to serve. But activists who are hoping that the federal government will support lifting the ban may have to wait a long time, Kiritsy contends, because many members of Congress and several presidential candidates have been unwilling to speak up against the policy. Meanwhile, the viewpoint concludes, the discriminatory ban compromises national security. Kiritsy is editor of BayWindows, *New England's largest gay, lesbian, bisexual, and transgendered newspaper.*

As you read, consider the following questions:

1. Who were the speakers on the Legacy of Service Tour, as described in the viewpoint?

Laura Kiritsy, "Discharged Soldier: 'Don't Ask, Don't Tell' Is Undermining U.S. Security," *Edge Boston*, August 23, 2007. Reproduced by permission.

2. How many gay, lesbian, bisexual and transgendered men and women are serving on active duty, according to estimates cited in the viewpoint?
3. In which Congressional body has there been more bipartisan support for the Military Readiness Enhancement Act, according to the viewpoint?

Taking an extremely narrow view of the war in Iraq, it could be said that one of the few positive things to arise from it has been the increased awareness of the absurdity of the U.S. military's anti-gay "Don't Ask, Don't Tell" policy....

At a panel discussion in Concord, New Hampshire, on Aug. 17, [2007,] former U.S. Army Sgt. Sonya Contreras, who served in Kosovo and then went on to be top recruiter, hit on the same theme, in a much more serious way. Her voice choked with emotion, Contreras, who was discharged in 2003 under "Don't Ask, Don't Tell," pitted the oft-stated argument that openly gay service members undermine troop morale against the current recruiting reality: "As a soldier first, it affects my morale to know that a known gang member can serve alongside other service members. As a woman, it affects my morale that a convicted rapist can serve alongside female service members. As a parent, it affects my morale that a convicted child molester can serve alongside military families. As Americans, it should affect all of our morale to know that Congress is forcing the U.S. military to choose convicted felons over competent, qualified and capable service members."

Contreras spoke as part of the Legacy of Service Tour, which features openly gay veterans who have served during the current war, discussing the toll of "Don't Ask, Don't Tell" on national security and on their own lives as part of the movement to repeal the policy. Joining her in the discussion at the Kimball Jenkins Estate Carriage House was retired Marine Staff Sgt. Eric Alva, who holds the unfortunate distinction of being the first U.S. service member wounded in the

Iraq War; Captain Antonio Agnone, a Marine who earned a commendation for leading a platoon that located and disarmed IEDs [improvised explosive devices] in Anbar province; Jarrod Chlapowski, a decorated Army linguist and Alexander Nicholson, an Arabic-speaking Army linguist discharged under "Don't Ask, Don't Tell" six months after 9/11. The discussion was moderated by Human Rights Campaign (HRC) President Joe Solmonese, whose organization is sponsoring the tour.

The tour hit New Hampshire, which [held] the country's pivotal first presidential primary early [in 2008], as the issue of repealing "Don't Ask, Don't Tell" increasingly becomes a topic of national discussion amidst a troop surge in Iraq and jockeying by 2008 presidential candidates.... In separate debates in New Hampshire back in June [2007]—clips of which were aired during the Legacy of Service discussion—Democratic and Republican candidates were asked to raise their hand if they supported lifting the ban. All of the Democratic candidates raised their hands; none of the Republicans did....

Agnone, who decided not to continue his service in the Marines in part because he was concerned that his partner, Brandon Suarez, would not be notified if Agnone was injured or killed in the line of duty, believes that Republican politicians who say "Don't Ask, Don't Tell" is working are either naive or just pandering to the GOP's anti-gay base.

"They say the policy is working simply because given the state of the Republican Party right now that's the only option that they have to say, that it's working, when it's clearly not." Citing activists' estimates that there are currently 65,000 LGBT [lesbian, gay, bisexual, and transgendered] troops on active duty, Agnone pointed out that the number is one-third of the active duty Marine Corps. The discharge of that many Marines on the armed services would be "absolutely devastating," Agnone asserted. "That's why we're in places like New Hampshire, that's why we've been in Iowa," Agnone told the crowd.

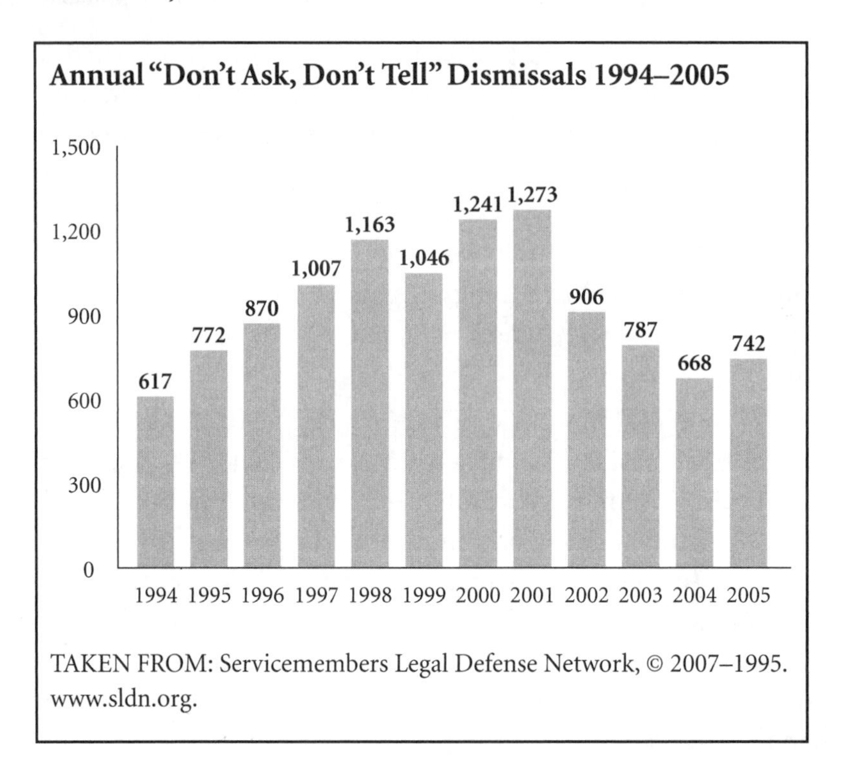

TAKEN FROM: Servicemembers Legal Defense Network, © 2007–1995. www.sldn.org.

"It's because you have the hands-on access to these candidates. And I'm asking you to let them know that when they say statements like that it's either proving that they're either completely dispassionate and have no idea what's going on the with the military or that they are just saying what needs to be said for political pandering."

LGBT activists are currently looking for a sponsor for legislation to repeal "Don't Ask, Don't Tell" in the U.S. Senate. The bill, known as the Military Readiness Enhancement Act (MREA), was introduced by former Bay State Congressman Marty Meehan in February [2007]. Despite the fact that they both support repealing the anti-gay policy, neither [Senator Hillary] Clinton or [Senator Barack] Obama have stepped forward to sponsor the bill—a fact Solmonese highlighted during the HRC/Logo forum when he asked Clinton why she hasn't yet filed the bill, which Meehan first introduced in 2005. Clinton, a member of the Senate Armed Services Committee, replied that "we didn't have a chance with the Republican Congress and George Bush as president." Now that there is a Democratic Congress, she said, there is discussion "about what steps we can take to sort of lay the groundwork so that when we do have a change in the White House, which can't happen too soon to suit me . . . we will be able to move on that." Clinton went on say that repealing the military policy is one of her "highest priorities."

In an interview with *Bay Windows* following the Legacy of Service discussion, Solmonese indicated that activists were more focused on finding a credible Republican to introduce the bill in the Senate. "We certainly know that both Senators Obama and [Clinton] will support whatever we do moving forward" regarding legislation to repeal "Don't Ask, Don't Tell," said Solmonese. But he also noted that "what the comprehensive leadership of that legislation looks like really matters. . . . That, as much as anything, has been the reason that we haven't moved forward on the Senate side." Unlike in the House, where there has been "healthy bipartisan support" for MREA, said Solmonese, "We haven't been able to get the Republican cosponsor on the Senate side that we would like to have."

Alva, who lost most of his right leg when he stepped on a landmine during the first day of the war, said that in the interest of national security, repealing the ban on openly gay service members needs to happen sooner rather than later. "Some of us up here are linguists, some of us were explosive ordinance officers, some of us were recruiters who sought out and put skilled men and women in the military and then were discharged because of who they were," said Alva, referring to his fellow panelists. "So a lot of us had valuable jobs and were very important to the armed forces. But because of that discriminatory policy, you're eliminating those factors of what is detrimental to our national security."

Periodical Bibliography

The following articles have been selected to supplement the diverse views presented in this chapter.

Aaron Belkin	"Don't Ask, Don't Tell: Does the Gay Ban Undermine the Military's Reputation?" *Armed Forces & Society*, January 2008.
Stephen Benjamin	"Don't Ask, Don't Translate," *New York Times*, June 8, 2007.
Joan Darrah	"A Call to Duty," September 10, 2007. www.advocate.com.
Elaine Donnelly	"General Pace and the PC Police," *Washington Times*, March 18, 2007.
Robert Fantina	"Republicans, Gays and the Military: Continued Prejudice," *American Chronicle*, January 16, 2008.
Nathaniel Frank	"Don't Need 'Don't Ask, Don't Tell,'" *Los Angeles Times*, December 4, 2007.
Marc Haeringer	"Coming Out in the Line of Fire," *Advocate*, July 3, 2007.
Michael Kinsley	"The Quiet Gay Revolution," *Time*, June 25, 2007.
Sarah Lyall	"Gay Britons Serve in Military With Little Fuss, as Predicted Discord Does not Occur," *New York Times*, May 21, 2007.
Irene Monroe	"Inclusion: Fighting the War at Home in the Military," *Black Commentator*, March 22, 2007. www.blackcommentator.com
John M. Shalikashvili	"Second Thoughts on Gays in the Military," *New York Times*, January 2, 2007.
Mark Thompson	"'Don't Ask, Don't Tell' Turns 15," *Time*, January 28, 2008.

CHAPTER 3

Should Same-Sex Couples Be Allowed to Marry?

Chapter Preface

On September 21, 1996 President Bill Clinton signed into law Pub. L. No. 104-199, 110 Stat. 2419, a law commonly known as the Defense of Marriage Act (DOMA). Under this law, the federal government was excused from offering any of the federal benefits of marriage to same-sex couples, even if they had been legally married in their home state. Further, the law guaranteed that if a married same-sex couple moved to another state, that new state would not have to recognize their marriage. The law kept the regulation of marriage as a right of the states, and prevented the federal government from getting involved in individual states' decisions. At the time, no state in the United States of America recognized same-sex couples in marriage, but the bill's sponsors wanted to make clear something they had always taken for granted: "that a marriage is the legal union of a man and a woman as husband and wife, and a spouse is a husband or wife of the opposite sex."

The new law was just part of an energetic debate that had been taking place since the Netherlands became the first country to recognize same-sex marriage in 2001. As other European nations also adopted same-sex marriage or a non-religious "civil union," many Americans watched anxiously for signs that the new policies might spread to North America. Many people, including a number of prominent religious organizations, campaigned actively against any recognition of same-sex marriage. The Alliance for Marriage, for example, argued on its Web site that "The benefits of marriage for husbands, wives, and children essentially and uniquely derive from the fact that marriage unites the two halves of the human race to share in raising children."

Evan Wolfson, father of the gay marriage movement, however, writes that same-sex couples "should be considered whole when they form a committed and loving relationship, as opposed to saying they are unwhole and unequal." Supporters of same-sex marriage point out, for example, that several states used to forbid marriage between white people and African Americans, using many of the same arguments that are used against same-sex marriage. In time, they argue, people learned to accept mixed-race families, just as they will learn to accept gay and lesbian couples.

Since the passage of DOMA, states have worked carefully through their legislatures and judicial bodies to clarify their positions on same-sex marriage. By 2008, only two states, Massachusetts and California, offered marriage equally to same-sex couples; four others had developed so-called civil unions, which grant many of the same legal rights as marriage but reserved the term "marriage" for unions sanctified by religious groups, generally understood to be for couples comprising one man and one woman. Four other states and the District of Columbia offered a legal union protecting some of the rights granted by marriage, but many fewer. And several states, alarmed by the 2004 action by Massachusetts to marry same-sex couples, amended their constitutions to prohibit marriages and civil unions in any form to same-sex couples.

But how people live as families and raise children is affected by more than just laws, and the questions cannot be fully answered by legislatures and judiciaries. In the following chapter, journalists, politicians, researchers, and parents examine how same-sex couples are changing our understanding of family life.

VIEWPOINT 1

"It would be the very height of foolishness to rely on the Supreme Court to protect marriage."

The United States Needs a Federal Marriage Amendment

Marilyn Musgrave

The following viewpoint was originally presented as a floor speech by Marilyn Musgrove, a Republican congresswoman from Colorado, during a debate over a proposed Federal Marriage Amendment in the United States House of Representatives. Musgrove argues that the best way to protect children is to protect the traditional notion of marriage through a constitutional amendment, and that such an amendment should be passed quickly before the tradition is further eroded. She points out that some states have already begun to recognize same-sex unions, and contends that the court system cannot be relied upon to safeguard marriage.

As you read, consider the following questions:

1. How did the Supreme Court describe marriage many years ago, according to the viewpoint?

Marilyn Musgrave, Floor Speech, *Congressional Record—House*, July 18, 2006, pp. H5298–5299.

2. As mentioned in the viewpoint, in which state did the Supreme Court decide the Goodridge case, legalizing same-sex marriage?
3. Why does our concern over a high divorce rate support the need for the Marriage Protection Amendment, according to the viewpoint?

Letters and e-mails and phone calls continue to pour into my office urging me to continue in this effort. We know that polls show that the overwhelming majority of the American people support traditional marriage, marriage between a man and a woman.

The people have a right to know whether their elected representatives agree with them about protecting traditional marriage.

I cannot think of a better good that this body may pursue than to promote and defend the idea that every child deserves both a father and a mother. Studies demonstrate the utmost importance of the presence of a child's biological parents in a child's happiness, health and future achievements. If we chip away at the institution which binds these parents and the family together, the institution of marriage, you begin to chip away at the future success of that child.

I would not want to negate the heroic job that many single parents do every day in providing the necessary support to a child's happiness. But today we are discussing what social policy is best for our children, and I am convinced that the best is found in promoting and defending traditional marriage.

Congress Should Act Now

Are there other important issues? Of course there are, but preserving the institution of marriage, which, as the Supreme Court said many years ago [in 1888] is "the foundation of the family and of society, without which there would be neither civilization nor progress," certainly warrants a few hours of our time. And even if there are other issues we need to address, as a former Member, one of my favorites, J.C. Watts said, "Members of Congress are capable of walking and chewing gum at the same time."

And where are those who say we are wasting time when we were renaming post offices and federal buildings earlier this year? Mr. Speaker, if we have enough time to rename post offices and federal buildings, surely we can spend one afternoon debating whether or not the traditional definition of marriage is worth preserving.

Others have asked why we need this amendment given that courts in New York, Georgia, and Nebraska have recently turned back challenges to traditional marriage. I just would like to say these decisions simply do not settle the issues. Cases in New Jersey and Washington, to name only two of many, remain pending.

Additionally, the Massachusetts Supreme Court's Goodridge decision legalizing same-sex marriage in that State continues to stand. Just last week, legislators in Massachusetts put off a measure to give the people the opportunity to decide this issue for themselves. While the Goodridge case remains on the books, court dockets all over the country will continue to be ensnarled with same-sex marriage litigation as opponents of traditional marriage continue to fight to expand their agenda to the rest of the country.

While recent court victories are not unimportant, the ultimate court test, the test in the United States Supreme Court, is still on the horizon. And legal experts agree at least four and probably five of the members of that court will act to overturn traditional marriage across America. That is why most legal experts expect DOMA [the 1996 Defense of Marriage Act] to fall once a challenge finally reaches the high court, which is why it would be the very height of foolishness to rely on the Supreme Court to protect marriage. Sadly, that

President Bush Calls for Constitutional Amendment

The Defense of Marriage requires a constitutional amendment. An amendment to the Constitution is never to be undertaken lightly. The amendment process has addressed many serious matters of national concern. And the preservation of marriage rises to this level of national importance. The union of a man and woman is the most enduring human institution, honoring—honored and encouraged in all cultures and by every religious faith. Ages of experience have taught humanity that the commitment of a husband and wife to love and to serve one another promotes the welfare of children and the stability of society.

Marriage cannot be severed from its cultural, religious and natural roots without weakening the good influence of society. Government, by recognizing and protecting marriage, serves the interests of all. Today I call upon the Congress to promptly pass, and to send to the states for ratification, an amendment to our Constitution defining and protecting marriage as a union of man and woman as husband and wife. The amendment should fully protect marriage, while leaving the state legislatures free to make their own choices in defining legal arrangements other than marriage.

Remarks by the President, Press Release from the Office of the Press Secretary. February 24, 2004.

August tribunal is part of the problem. Justice [Antonin] Scalia has already warned us that the Court's 2003 *Lawrence* decision was only the beginning of a road at the end of which is a radical redefinition of marriage at the hands of the Court.

Does anyone else see the irony in the opponents of this bill calling on us to wait until the Supreme Court rules before deciding this issue? Many of those who protested the loudest that DOMA was unconstitutional when it was enacted in 1996 are today the ones who say we ought to presume DOMA is constitutional until the high court tells us otherwise.

Marriage Laws Should Protect Children

The American people want us to settle this issue now. They don't want us to wait to see how much havoc the courts will wreak on the definition of marriage before we act to protect it.

Our marriage laws represent centuries of cumulative wisdom regarding the best way to address public concerns about property, inheritance, legal liability and raising children. The last matter is especially important because we now know beyond any reasonable doubt that children thrive best when they are raised in a traditional family. And statistically speaking, the further we go from this ideal, the more we can expect to see increases in measures of a whole host of social problems.

Again, this is not to say that children raised in non-traditional families will necessarily fall prey to these problems, but public policy is based on cumulative, not individual experience. Facts, as it has been said, are stubborn things. And one sad but stubborn fact is that the statistical dice are loaded against children who are raised without a father and a mother.

Some oppose the Marriage Protection Amendment on the grounds that the institution of marriage is already in trouble. Why be concerned, they say, about same-sex marriage when the divorce rate among couples in traditional marriages is so high? But can't you see this is a non sequitur? It is like saying to a doctor: The patient already has pneumonia, so why are you taking precautions to prevent him from getting a staph infection? Yes, traditional marriage has its problems, we all know that, and the high divorce rate is a national scandal. But far from undermining my point, this reinforces it. We are dismayed by the breakup of families because we know broken families lead to more and more children being deprived of the tremendous benefit of having both their mom and dad around to raise them.

Other opponents of this amendment argue that the existence of same-sex marriage in Massachusetts has not caused the earth to stop spinning on its axis, so they ask what is all this fuss about. After only two years of experience, it is absurd to suggest that we can even begin to guess how the redefinition of marriage in that State will ramify in the future. And the fact that same-sex marriages in Massachusetts do not directly affect my marriage or your marriage means nothing in regard to the public policy debate. The breakup of the family next door does not directly affect your marriage or my marriage either, but we all recognize that every family that comes apart is a tragedy, and that is why our laws have always sought to encourage, not undermine, traditional families.

VIEWPOINT 2

> *"The Constitution was never intended to set social policy."*

The United States Does Not Need a Federal Marriage Amendment

Charles Krauthammer

In the following viewpoint, Charles Krauthammer argues that congressional debate over a constitutional amendment banning same-sex marriage is a waste of energy. While he opposes the state of Massachusetts's decision to recognize same-sex marriages, he contends that laws already in place will slow the spread of such recognition. He concludes that when judicial activists overstep their bounds, as they have done in recognizing same-sex couples, the solution is to remove them, not to change the Constitution, and to elect presidents who will appoint right-thinking Supreme Court justices. Krauthammer is a Pulitzer Prize-winning syndicated columnist and commentator whose work regularly appears in national publications.

As you read, consider the following questions:

1. How many more votes would the U.S. Senate have needed to pass a constitutional amendment banning same-sex marriage, as reported in the viewpoint?

2. According to the viewpoint, which law protects a state that does not allow same-sex marriage from having to recognize same-sex marriages performed in other states?
3. What are the two purposes of the Constitution, according to the author?

On Wednesday [June 7, 2006] the Senate fell eighteen votes short of the two-thirds majority that would have been required to pass a constitutional amendment banning gay marriage. The mainstream media joined Sen. Edward Kennedy in calling the entire debate a distraction from the nation's business and a wedge with which to divide Americans.

Since the main business of Congress is to devise ever more ingenious ways (earmarked and non-earmarked) to waste taxpayers' money, any distraction from the main business is welcome. As for dividing Americans, who came up with the idea of radically altering the most ancient of all social institutions in the first place? Until the past few years, every civilization known to man has defined marriage as between people of opposite sex. To charge with "divisiveness" those who would do nothing more than resist a radical overturning of that norm is a sign of either gross partisanship or serious dimwittedness.

And that partisanship and dimwittedness obscured the rather interesting substance of the recent Senate debate. It revolved around the two possible grounds for the so-called Marriage Protection Amendment: federalism and popular sovereignty.

Federalism

When one state, such as Massachusetts, adopts gay marriage, the full-faith-and-credit clause of the Constitution might reasonably be applied to require other states to recognize such marriages, and thus, essentially force it upon the rest of the nation. Federalism, however, is meant to allow states the au-

The Colonialists and Marriage

Massachusetts' history reminds us that what we commonly call marriage today was initially, and quite deliberately, constructed as a form of civil union.

In every region of colonial North America, devout believers fought over how to define true religion, and where to draw the line between church and state. In some of the smaller and initially more homogeneous colonies like Massachusetts and Connecticut, religious uniformity was enforced by the state. But taken collectively, no single religion in colonial America ever had the power to decide for everyone, everywhere, what was sacred. As a practical matter, the traditional practice of state-enforced religious uniformity proved to be unworkable in the new American republic. It was this *de facto* diversity that the First Amendment to the U.S. Constitution enshrined in federal law.

Mark A. Peterson, "Civil Unions in the City on a Hill," Common-Place, *vol. 4, no. 3, April 2004. www.common-place.org.*

tonomy of social experimentation (as with Oregon's legalization of assisted suicide) from which other states can learn. It is not intended to force other states to follow.

But it turns out that the Massachusetts experiment has not been forced on other states. No courts have required other states to recognize gay marriages performed in Massachusetts. Gay activists have not pushed it, wisely calculating that it would lead to a huge backlash. Moreover, Congress's Defense of Marriage Act (DOMA) explicitly prevents the state-to-state export of gay marriage.

Should DOMA be overturned, that would justify a constitutional amendment to prevent one state from imposing its will on the other forty-nine. But it has not been overturned.

And under the current Supreme Court, it is unlikely to be. The Marriage Protection Amendment is therefore superfluous.

Popular Sovereignty

That leaves justification No. 2:

Popular Sovereignty. Gay marriage is a legitimate social issue to be decided democratically. The problem is that imperial judges are legislating their personal preferences, striking down popular will and calling it constitutional law.

Most notoriously, in Massachusetts a total of four judges out of seven decided that the time had come for gay marriage. More recently, in Georgia and Nebraska, judges have overturned (state) constitutional amendments banning gay marriage that had passed with more than 70 percent of the vote.

This is a rerun of the abortion fiasco: judicial fiat that decades later leaves the issue roilingly unsettled and divisive. This is no way to set social policy in a democracy. So why not have a federal constitutional amendment and smite the arrogant solons of Massachusetts, Nebraska and Georgia, and those yet to come, all at once?

Because it is an odd solution for a popular-sovereignty problem to take the gay-marriage issue completely out of the hands of the people. Once the constitutional amendment is passed, should the current ethos about gay marriage change, no people in any state could ever permit gay marriage.

Judicial Overreaching

The amendment actually ends up defeating the principle it sets out to uphold. The solution to judicial overreaching is to change the judiciary, not to undo every act of judicial arrogance with a policy-specific constitutional amendment. Where does it end? Yesterday it was school busing and abortion. Today it is flag burning and gay marriage.

It won't end until the Constitution becomes pockmarked with endless policy amendments. The Constitution was never intended to set social policy. Its purpose is to (a) establish the rules of governance and (b) secure for the individual citizen rights against the power of the state. It defaces the Constitution to turn it into a super-legislative policy document.

In the short run, judicial arrogance is to be fought democratically with the means still available. Rewording and repassing the constitutional amendment in Georgia, for example. Appealing the Nebraska decision right up to the Supreme Court, which, given its current composition, is extremely likely to terminate with prejudice this outrageous example of judicial interposition.

In the longer run, it means having Supreme Courts that routinely strike down such judicial imperialism. And that means electing presidents who nominate [conservative Supreme Court Justices] John Roberts and Sam Alito rather than [liberal Justices] Stephen Breyer and Ruth Bader Ginsburg.

True, this does nothing about today's judicial usurpation in Massachusetts. But that is the problem of its good citizens. If they want to, they have the power to amend their own state constitution. In the meantime, Massachusetts remains quarantined by DOMA.

Therefore, there is no need (yet) to disfigure the U.S. Constitution with a policy amendment.

VIEWPOINT 3

"I remain in favor of 'civil unions' as a concept . . . less tilted toward the equating of gay and heterosexual unions."

Civil Unions Are a Reasonable Alternative to Marriage for Same-Sex Couples

Dennis O'Brien

In the following viewpoint, Dennis O'Brien explains that he prefers to grant same-sex couples civil unions than the right to marry. He agrees with those who favor legal recognition for these couples, because he values fidelity, but he contends that same-sex couples deny themselves the spiritual expansion that heterosexual couples experience. He concludes that offering equal marriage sends the dangerous message to children that heterosexual and homosexual partnerships are also equal. O'Brien is a philosopher and the former president of the University of Rochester. He is the author of The Idea of a Catholic University *(2002).*

As you read, consider the following questions:

1. Which clause of the Vermont constitution was violated by denying gay and lesbian couples marital rights, according to the Vermont Supreme Court?

Dennis O'Brien, "A More Perfect Union," The *Christian Century*, vol. 121, January 27, 2004, pp. 27–31.

2. According to the viewpoint, what evidence is there that heterosexual marriage can be unsuccessful?
3. How do Americans tend to view the reasons for law, according to the viewpoint?

We have a bumper sticker on our car: "Keep Vermont Civil." The sticker is a bit tattered, since it goes back to the controversy about "civil unions"—the Vermont law passed in 2000 establishing various legal equivalences to marital rights for gay and lesbian couples. The legislature had been forced to take action following the 1999 ruling of the Vermont Supreme Court holding that denial of marital rights to such unions violated the Vermont constitution's "common benefits" clause.

In a neat bit of Solomonic judgment, the court both rejected the gay and lesbian plaintiffs' claim that they were entitled to marriage licenses and declared that they were entitled to the benefits "incident on the marital relation." The court ruled that those benefits could be established by granting a marriage license, but that there might be other legislative means to assure proper benefits. The matter of specific statute was handed over to the legislature. The result was "civil unions."

A ruling in November 2003 by the Supreme Judicial Court of Massachusetts similarly affirmed "marital" rights for gay and lesbian couples and handed the matter on to the legislature of the Commonwealth. The tone of the 4-3 decision of the Massachusetts Court appears, however, to push toward an unequivocal affirmation of "gay marriage." That would seem to be the hope and expectation of gay activists. Perhaps "gay marriage" will finally emerge as the statutory provision as it has in Canada and in various European jurisdictions. The heavens will not fall, the republic will not totter if that is the direction of public policy, but I am not enthusiastic about such a result. I prefer the "civil unions" approach. . . .

The real issues about sexuality are choice, lifestyle and cultural value. On the basis of genes or Freudian polymorphous sex, sexuality in many forms is a fact. The question is: How should society assess and shape various sexual expressions? Is America now more morally sensitive, more well structured in its laws and practices insofar as it accepts publicly avowed homosexual behavior; constructs laws that protect homosexuals from the criminal penalties formally attached to homosexual acts; and allows for civil unions or even gay marriages? On the whole, I am inclined to say that getting gay sex out of the closet and legally protected is a moral and political advance. But that is not because homosexuality is natural but because something of value emerges from it. . . .

Cultural Realities

One of the confusions in the sexual polemics of the day is the blurring of the line between natural orientation and chosen behavior. If you have the orientation, then of course behavior should follow and is fully morally legitimate. Sexual libertarians argue that the repression of sexual urges of whatever sort is psychologically disastrous and culturally stultifying. I like this argument because it shifts to issues of moral choice and social values. Repression is bad for you and your society!

Just how far should the value of non-repression be taken? One of the byproducts of the sexual revolution has been the emergence of bisexuality—presumably a natural given. Advocates of marriage, heterosexual or gay, would both have to agree that bisexual orientation must be repressed in the interests of marital fidelity. One cannot be faithful to a sexual partner if one is having sex with someone of a different sex. Gay marriage advocates are, as they often say, conservatives on the issue of sexual fidelity. . . .

Any argument for heterosexuality as a preferred sexual choice does not rest on how this or that heterosexual life works out. Heterosexual marriage can be a human disaster—

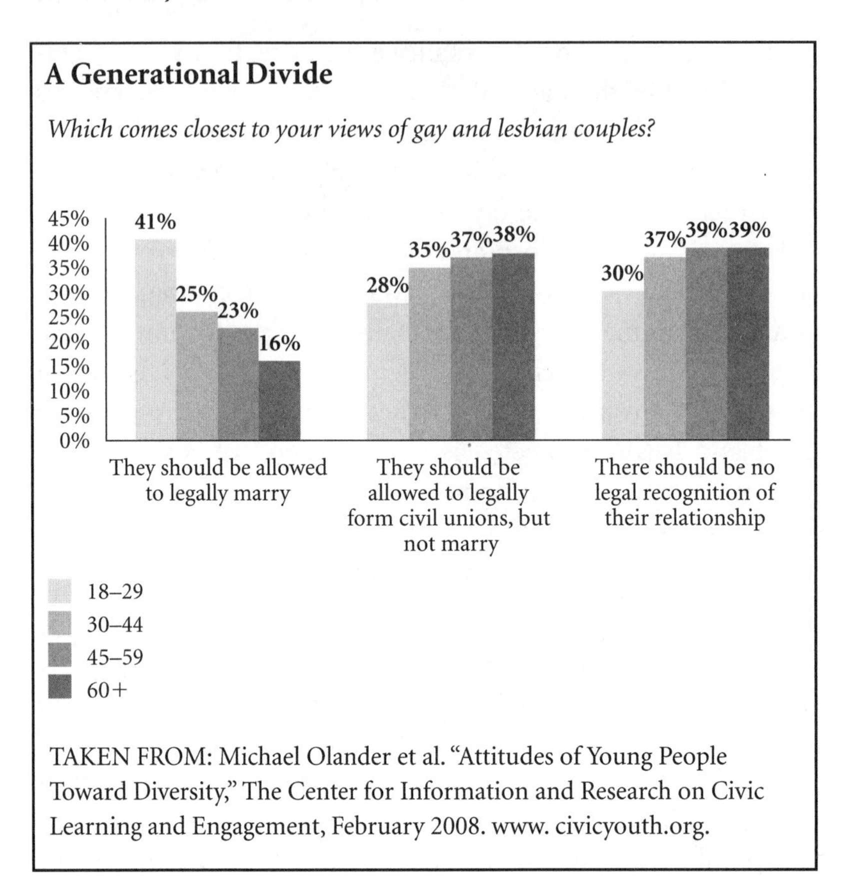

TAKEN FROM: Michael Olander et al. "Attitudes of Young People Toward Diversity," The Center for Information and Research on Civic Learning and Engagement, February 2008. www. civicyouth.org.

the divorce statistics attest to that! Homosexual bonding may be deeply valuable and, as noted, reach ranges of the human heart that heterosexuality cannot. Any argument for heterosexuality must deal with broad cultural and spiritual realities.

Having said that, it is obvious that constructing the case for heterosexuality must be as complex and nuanced as the cultural and spiritual trajectories of the human spirit. To short-circuit that long argument, I would say that it comes down to the ancient belief that men and women are different. Luce Irigary puts it well in *An Ethics of Sexual Difference*: "man and woman, woman and man are always meeting as though for the first time because they cannot be substituted for one another."

Why heterosexuality? Because the human spirit can expand as it moves toward the different. It can; it may not. Certainly some homosexual (or celibate) life choices arise from a fear of the different in women (or men). On the other hand, in a society that devalues heterosexuality and marriage through a mix of sentimentality and sexual titillation, the choice of homosexuality may be the choice of the different which is revelatory. So be it. But the final fact is that the bodily, biological difference between men and women is the urtext of the heterosexual narrative. Writing that sexual script is inherently difficult—that is the reason that sentimentality and fantasy are so popular: they conceal the pain of difference and the lessons of loving across that pain.

The Role of the Law

One might well conclude that commending heterosexuality as a preferred sexual life is educationally legitimate, and then ask: But what about the law? Just because one may commend one life choice over another—being a social worker over being a stockbroker—does not mean the preference needs to be legally enforced (there is no law against being a stockbroker). Perhaps the issue of gay or heterosexual direction should be left to the subtleties of parental or church guidance. Whether that is the final conclusion or not will depend on how one views the role of law.

For classical philosophers law had an educational function; it was set up to structure individual and communal life in order to produce certain human virtues. In Aristotle's work, *The Nichomachean Ethics* and the *Politics* are mutually supporting. One needs certain virtues like courage, temperance and justice in order to realize human good, but those virtues are also necessary to be a good citizen. The state, in turn, is bound through the enactment and enforcement of proper laws to educate for virtue both for its own sake and for human prospering.

The educational role of law is at best recessive in the American understanding of law. We tend to view law not as aimed at creating individual or common good but as a means of mediating dispute and keeping civil peace. In so far as that is the dominant view of law in America, "gay marriage" says nothing about the morality of homosexuality one way or the other, it simply guarantees that all "domestic partnerships" (an alternative term considered for "civil unions") are treated equally. All well and good. But I am not certain that one can ever completely erase the educational effect of law.

The law may not deliberately create culture, but it certainly becomes a sign within the culture. Giving legal status to gay marriage does appear to suggest that the difference between gay and heterosexual partnerships is a matter of irrelevance. It will surely make it more difficult for parents or the churches to argue a preference for heterosexual marriage (which I hope they will wish to do). Thus I remain in favor of "civil union" as a concept more in keeping with our restrained sense of law and less tilted toward the equating of gay and heterosexual unions.

VIEWPOINT 4

> *"More companies would provide health benefits to gay families if the legal designation changed to 'married.'"*

Civil Unions Are Not a Reasonable Alternative to Marriage

Norma Love

In the following viewpoint, journalist Norma Love lists several ways in which New Hampshire's civil unions law, which came into effect on January 1, 2008, is inadequate. While it does expand the rights and benefits of same-sex couples living in the state, she argues, it cannot extend federal benefits to same-sex couples, and gay and lesbian couples who move outside the state may not be legally recognized. While civil unions are a step forward, she concludes, only a legal right to marriage will provide true equality. Love covers state government and politics in New Hampshire for The Associated Press.

As you read, consider the following questions:

1. How many federal laws will discriminate against couples joined by a civil union in New Hampshire, according to the viewpoint?

Norma Love, "N.H. Civil Unions: Legal Protections, Obligations and Pitfalls," December 30, 2007. www.phillyburbs.com. Reproduced by permission.

2. As reported in the viewpoint, which three companies are among the many that offer benefits to the partners of gay employees?
3. Why did New Hampshire Governor John Lynch sign his state's law recognizing civil unions, according to the viewpoint?

New Hampshire's new civil unions law, though well-intentioned, makes a promise to gay couples it can't keep: that all the rights, obligations and responsibilities of marriage will be theirs.

In fact, they will not be treated equally, either inside New Hampshire or beyond its borders.

They will fall into a separate, evolving legal class recognized by only a handful of states. And more than 1,100 federal laws will discriminate against them regardless of where they live.

Gay couples taking advantage of the law, which takes effect Tuesday, [January 1, 2008] indeed acquire substantial new state protections ranging from important health benefits to the ability to inherit without a will.

But they will be treated legally as two unmarried adults in all but New Jersey, Vermont, Connecticut and California. They probably will be recognized in Oregon, whose domestic partner law was to take effect Tuesday [January 1, 2008] but a federal judge put the law on hold last Friday [December 28, 2007] pending a February hearing requested by opponents.

Their status isn't as clear in Massachusetts, the only state that allows same-sex marriage, nor in Washington, Maine, Hawaii and the District of Columbia, which recognize domestic partners to varying degrees.

Adding to the legal confusion, gay couples moving to New Hampshire and getting united may still face questions about their status. For example, just released New Hampshire Insurance Department guidelines recognize, without question, health insurance policies subject to Oregon law, but those from California only on a case-by-case basis.

Federal Laws Do Not Recognize Gay Couples

Even if they never leave New Hampshire, couples united under the new law won't have the same rights or receive the same benefits that heterosexual couples enjoy under federal laws. They are specifically excluded under the 1996 federal Defense of Marriage Act, which defines marriage as between one man and one woman. Many states have adopted similar laws.

Gay couples united in New Hampshire, or any other state, won't qualify for federal Social Security or veterans survivor benefits or be able to sponsor a foreign national to immigrate as their spouse.

Federal laws governing multi-state employer health plans will continue to allow the companies to discriminate against their united gay employees. Such discrimination will be illegal under state-regulated health plans that cover married couples.

Also, united gay couples will pay taxes on most if not all of the value of costlier health insurance plans, a cost not passed on to married couples. Unlike married heterosexual couples, united gay couples cannot file joint federal income tax returns.

Another potential downside faces couples who come to New Hampshire to enter civil unions. They run the risk of being locked in legal limbo if they return home to a state that doesn't recognize their status. A similar problem faces New Hampshire couples who move away.

Employers May Not Recognize Gay Couples

More than 9,300 companies already cover gay couples, including The Associated Press, UPS and Verizon. Though that number is growing, many companies still do not extend benefits.

Gay couples with one member working for the state or local government in New Hampshire now will get the same

"I Now Pronounce You Legally Meaningless Man and Same Sex Partner," cartoon by Clive Goodard. www.cartoonstock.com.

pension benefits as their heterosexual counterparts. But gay couples that include a federal employee won't get the same recognition under the federal retirement system.

Gay couples won't pay state taxes to transfer property from one partner to the other, but they could be liable for federal gift taxes.

In short, legal experts say couples should see a lawyer before entering into a union, or at least check with their employer's benefits department so they aren't surprised at being taxed or disappointed at being excluded. They also should keep, and carry out of state, legal documents that married couples might not need, such as ones allowing each other to make medical decisions if one is incapacitated.

"Everything couples did before to protect themselves, they should do after a civil union," said Michele Granda, a staff attorney for Boston-based Gay & Lesbian Advocates & Defenders, or GLAD.

"It really is a level of fairness that is long overdue, but there are holes in the safety net," she said. "It's a step, but it can't be a stop. It's opened the door to a future of possibilities but it will not provide the equality that many people think it will."

Promises Enforced

The benefits can be substantial, however.

Lara Schwartz, legal director for the Human Rights Campaign, said New Hampshire's law in particular provides important protections for couples and children when one spouse dies or the couple divorces.

"It's basically the state enforcing your promises to one another," she said.

Unlike heterosexual marriage, civil unions are not universally recognized, however, which can make entering into one far easier than getting out of one.

New Hampshire has no waiting period for a civil union regardless of residency. Nor is there a waiting period for divorce if both are residents. But if only one of the divorcing parties is a resident, he or she must wait one year.

John Rich, a Manchester attorney, said residents who have homes in another state but retain New Hampshire as their official domicile should be able to get a divorce. Couples who move and break their ties to New Hampshire may experience the dilemma facing a gay Rhode Island couple that married in Massachusetts: a requirement that one move to Massachusetts for a year to dissolve the marriage.

"When you cross state lines, there's a question whether your family exists at all," Schwartz said.

Vermont Reconsiders Civil Unions

Seven years after enacting the nation's first civil unions law, Vermont is asking the public if same-sex marriage would provide more equity.

Thomas Little, chairman of the Vermont Commission on Family Recognitions and Protection, said the most frequent complaint at hearings is that federal law doesn't recognize gay unions. That wouldn't change if Vermont allowed same-sex marriage, he said.

But Middlebury attorney Beth Robinson, chairwoman of the Vermont Freedom to Marry Task Force, argues that more companies would provide health benefits to gay families if the legal designation changed to "married." More importantly, the designation would provide stronger legal grounds to sue for full recognition, Robinson said.

New Hampshire Gov. John Lynch said he hasn't analyzed what other states have done or what impact his state's law will have on them. He signed the law to end discrimination and protect families, he said.

"I think we've done the right thing in New Hampshire and that's the state I'm primarily worried about," Lynch said.

Despite the limitations of civil unions, New Hampshire expects 3,500 to 4,000 couples to get them in the first year.

Some, like Jeff Burr, 49, and Neil Blair, 44, of Franconia, want to put faces to the law.

"Yes, it's about the civil rights, but it's also about the whole civil rights movement. It's about the big picture. It's about the journey. It's about doing what's right," said Blair.

Others, like Betsy Peabody, 46, and Dianne Harhigh, 49, of Concord, want to legally strengthen their family by making a stepparent adoption possible. Harhigh plans to adopt Peabody's 6-year-old daughter, Julia.

Peabody is a realist. She knows civil unions aren't the same as marriage.

"I'm OK with forward motion even if it's not where we want to be. It's not realistic to get to where we want to be without steps along the way," she said.

VIEWPOINT 5

> *"Marriage is supposed to mean ... one man, one woman, formally and officially joined in the hope of becoming a real family."*

Civil Unions Pose a Threat to the Institution of Marriage

Midge Decter

In the following viewpoint, Midge Decter argues that allowing same-sex couples to form civil unions is not a reasonable compromise, but rather a direct assault on the natural and moral concept of marriage. Many gay men and women, she contends, are not so interested in marrying as they are in attacking the way heterosexuals live. Appropriately, the oppression of gay men and women in our society has nearly stopped, she concludes, but granting civil unions is going too far. Decter is an author and social critic, and a member of the boards of trustees of the conservative Heritage Foundation and the Institute on Religion and Public Life.

As you read, consider the following questions:

1. How did the Civil Rights Movement influence the gay rights movement, according to the viewpoint?

Midge Decter, "Stop Compromising on 'Civil Unions'," *USA Today*, vol. 135, March 2007, pp. 52–53.

2. As the author explains it, why do lesbian couples tend to be more successful than couples of gay men?
3. According to the viewpoint, why does the author oppose a constitutional amendment banning same-sex marriage?

The term "civil marriage" or "civil union" has become a euphemism for the legal and social legitimation of homosexuality. In current public conversation, the phrase no longer means the wedding of a man and woman conducted by a civil authority—a town clerk, justice of the peace, or judge. In that old sense of the term, of course, every legal marriage is a civil one, because the ministers, priests, and rabbis who conduct weddings according to the established rites of their respective religions are at the same time acting with full civil authority to do so. The fact that so many of the fully sanctioned marriages in recent years have turned out to be too casual and thin-blooded to hold out for very long against the trials of real life is nothing to the point. For while the number of easy-come, easy-go marriages in our midst speaks to the failure of spiritual education in this great, rich, lucky, but somewhat spiritually impoverished land of ours, there has not, until now, been any kind of real assault on what marriage is supposed to mean: one man, one woman, formally and officially joined in the hope of becoming a real family.

Today, what is being called "civil marriage" is a kind of trick of language, a term used as a political euphemism for surrendering to the most recent demand of the homosexual rights movement. What it now is intended to mean is that the mating of two men or two women must be regarded by society as equally hallowed. The surrender to this idea has taken place very quickly, and I think we cannot understand it without going over the history of how we got here.

Homosexual rights is an idea that began to assume the force and energy of a movement hard on the heels of the women's movement (which itself, of course, gained energy and force from the civil rights movement that preceded it). It began with the demand that homosexuals no longer be considered pariahs, bedeviled by the authorities and viewed with unconcealed discomfort by many of their fellow citizens. In the abstract, this demand seemed very reasonable, particularly among people still stung by the shame of the country's long history of attitude and behavior toward blacks. The movement was what you might call a smash success—perhaps because it was the third in a row and thus was presenting its case to an already softened public, or perhaps because to assent quickly to the movement's claims made it a lot easier to avert one's eyes from homosexuality itself. In any case, rapid is the word.

In the years since the homosexual movement began, the country had been confronted with the phenomenon of AIDS, a mortal disease that, at the beginning of the epidemic, was contracted in one of two ways: either a common form of homosexual mating or the use of dirty needles for injecting heroin. AIDS, it will be remembered, for a time virtually was threatening to decimate the male homosexual community. Though at first there was a good deal of lying about the problem—"We are all at risk," said the sympathizers and those raising funds for medical research to find a cure—the lie could not be sustained for long. Heroin addicts, prostitutes, and recipients of tainted blood aside, among homosexuals it was, and is, spread through a kind of blind and rampant promiscuity that had been growing ever more so in certain institutions, primarily the bars and bathhouses.

In any case, what the misguided enablers were revving up to embrace, Mother Nature obdurately was rejecting. The impulse of compassion for the discriminated against had become so habitual that, rather than expressions of horror, what the discovery of AIDS elicited from the community of the sensitive was a great outpouring of sympathy. Though AIDS was a disease contracted by a species of sexual behavior that might have straightened the curls of many a fashionable lady to hear about, the issue was spoken of in polite circles as a kind of mysterious tragedy that struck out of the blue. Men dying of the disease were not merely pitied, but positively beautified among the artistic community in song and story—song and story, indeed, in which the word "angels" figured heavily.

Now, obviously, there are homosexuals who are not and never have been activists, who do not storm the streets, who do not frequent the bathhouses, and who keep their sex lives—as most of the rest of us do—to themselves. Yet, in the current debate, these homosexuals, are, alas, irrelevant. They neither are the stuff of which movements and flamboyant public gestures are made, nor are they people whose ambition is to overturn the conditions of ordinary, everyday life.

[In 1996,] Congress passed the Defense of Marriage Act, which states in so many words that marriage is a union between one man and one woman. Imagine a congressional act that certifies something—more properly, reminds us of something—that one might have thought should need no reminding. The members of Congress who proposed, and then passed, this act were defending marriage from the already looming demand that it be redefined to include homosexual coupledom. As we now know, the act was insufficient to hold off the assault from the idea that marriage be defined as an act of commitment between any two people of whatever sex.

Many of the leading defenders of marriage in the land had proposed that we—at least the citizens of three-quarters of the states—include among the articles of the Constitution a statement that denies definitely the demand that homosexuals be granted the legal right to marry. Thus doth compassion, combined with a certain willful blindness, make cowards of us all. A culture grown sick with the refusal to uphold common wisdom—and common sense—sinks to requiring the services of politics and politicians in the face of difficulty. (The amendment ultimately was defeated, however.)

Marriage Measure a Shaky Solution

Outside the [Massachusetts] State House last week [in March 2004] the passion over gay marriage was clear.

But inside the House chamber, the tedious legislative process had ground the drama into a mushy compromise that no one loves.

Lawmakers appeared reluctant to embrace the measure, which would ban gay marriage and create civil unions for gay couples. . . .

Among lawmakers and interest groups, liberals don't like the compromise because they view civil unions as falling far short of the promise of gay marriage that was established by the Supreme Judicial Court. Conservatives don't like it because they see civil unions as equivalent to marriage for same-sex couples.

The architects of the amendment say the fact that neither the political left nor right has embraced the compromise demonstrates its beauty.

Rick Klein,
"Marriage Measure a Shaky Solution,"
Boston Globe, *March 14, 2004.*

Because the question of homosexual marriage has, at this time, been left in the hands of judges—mere legislation having proved to be of little avail against the forces of activism—we have been treated to the sight of homosexual couples celebrating outside of courthouses and city halls in such places as San Francisco, Boston, and Trenton. By the way and, not surprisingly, it seems that a number of the male couples have admitted they had no intention of getting married—it merely was their having won the battle that they were there to celebrate—while every one of the female couples declared their intention to marry. I say not surprisingly because—some might think it impolite of me to point out—homosexual men essentially are no more like lesbians than heterosexual men are like the women whom they either merely pursue or marry. In short, men are men and women are women, whatever their sexual proclivities—which brings us to the nature of modern, that is to say, voluntary, marriage.

In the contemporary world, marriage is the result of a voluntary agreement between two people that they will swear to make a home together and be faithful to one another. It is, in other words, a deal. Cleave unto me, says the man, and I will cherish and protect you; cleave unto me, says the woman, and I will make your life comfortable, bear your children, and be faithful to you. Of course, this deal is sometimes—nowadays, indeed, fearfully often—honored in the breach. Nevertheless, it is the best arrangement ever devised for those, meaning all of us, who are considerably lower than the angels. Moreover, it is not merely happenstance that so very large a number of these deals are consecrated by formal ritual in houses of worship, where they are blessed in the name, not only of the state, but of God.

Female homosexuals who have achieved coupledom tend to approximate this arrangement far more closely than do male homosexuals—even those male homosexuals who remain together for life (and who are, by the way, much fewer in number). This is because—again—women are different from men. They wish—correction; need—to be monogamous and faithful; it is in their nature. Men, on the other hand, in the most elementary sense of the nature of males, have impulses to promiscuity. A woman says to her prospective mate, "Be faithful to me and I promise that I will make it worth your while." It is a bargain men who marry not only agree to but, in a very important sense, are saved by. Being women, lesbians most often are given to a facsimile of this same deal. Moreover, they can be, and often are, mothers and thus inclined to stability. Men who are sexually attracted to, and even truly love, other men have no such exchange to make. In an all-male society, rampant sex is the norm. As things have grown easier and more comfortable for men to be openly, often flagrantly, homosexual in our overly tolerant society, the recklessness of the bathhouse and orgy has become the norm. Hence, for example, the wildfire of HIV and AIDS (and now, I am told, certain even newer forms of venereal disease). That is why the right to marriage, fought for with every weapon at their command by homosexual men, would—or, must I say, will—largely be acted on by lesbians.

Why, then, are these men fighting so hard for it? The answer is, the right to legal marriage that they are demanding is not about them—it is about the rest of us. It is, and is meant to be, a spit in the eye of the way we live. Whatever the variety of efforts to oppose it—another law or even an entire set of laws, let's say, or a constitutional amendment—none of it will matter unless, and until, all the nice and decent people in the United States begin to understand that we are in a crisis, and it is up to them to sustain and, with all good cheer, defend the way they lead their lives.

Defiling the Constitution

The proposed constitutional amendment was not a good idea because I fear the oh-so-easy use of that great document to deal with problems that arise from this society's sloth and unwillingness to face the mess that has become of our culture in general and the issue of sex and family in particular. It would be a shame if we had to tinker with so rare and precious an inheritance as our Constitution because people who hate the way we live storm the streets while others try to look away. Also, we should keep in mind the nature of politicians. A key part of their job is to keep people happy. Indeed, doing so is the way most of them got that job in the first place. That is why only a very few moral heroes among them risk being frowned at by their constituents or, worse, making them angry. There is no sense in anyone's complaining about this; it is in the nature of our political system—and it is the best system that has yet been devised by man. However, politicians simply do not—indeed, cannot—make useful arbiters of cultural problems, let alone spiritual ones, like this.

Let me return to the idea being proposed by some that we invent a kind of second-level marriage—call it "civil union"—that would provide homosexual couples with certain legal and financial marital rights without the full standing of heterosexual marriage. I am not against allowing a homosexual to be his partner's legal heir, for instance, or to be granted official status as rightful partner in a hospital emergency room or other such things. Yet, this idea of creating a new level of marriage—call it whatever you want—smacks of the congenital passion of politicians to invent a compromise where none will serve. For it is not compromise that the homosexual rights movement is after, nor do they even want the standing in the community that heterosexuals have. They are radicals. What they want is not a room of their own; they want to bring the whole house down.

By now, we, as a society, pretty much have ceased the persecution of homosexuals. They are not ostracized from polite society. (If truth be told, many of them never were.) They freely camp around to a most appreciative audience on prime-time television and, as we know, have for some time served as the arbiters of high fashion. In New York, they have a high school that has become an official part of the city's public school system, and though they have been seen on the newscasts standing outside California, Massachusetts, and New Jersey courthouses smiling and waving their new marriage licenses, it is vitally important to remember that they are the denizens of a radical movement.

So, if I am against a constitutional amendment and oppose unequivocally the idea of civil union, what do I wish? I want us to stick up for ourselves and the way we live, be as mighty a force in the culture as we are entitled to be if nothing else by virtue of our sheer numbers. I want us to resist all attacks on the way we live, whether from our kids and grandchildren, their momentary culture heroes, or from the overpaid, mindless, sheeplike followers of fashion in the press and academic community who make so much noise in the world around us every day. In other words, let's take back our country. Let us be decent, civil, and even loving to our homosexual fellow citizens, but draw the line on what they stand for and on everything else that makes light of our existence.

For the privilege of living in the most nobly founded, freest, and richest country in the world, we owe nothing less, not only to ourselves, but to the oncoming tide of generations. We are given the choice of leaving them with a blessing or a curse. Not so many people in the world have that choice. I hope we can go down in history as having deserved it.

> *"The more I examine marriage, the more obvious it becomes that the laws are written to favor a certain two-by-two lifestyle that is simply a fiction."*

The Institution of Marriage Itself Is Out of Date

Mary E. Hunt

In the following viewpoint, Mary E. Hunt considers the arguments for and against same-sex marriage, and concludes that the practice of allowing the government to regulate family relationships should be done away with. Marriage grants two people—whether of the same or of different sexes—rights and benefits that are not extended to different configurations of successful and caring families. Churches should feel free to bless particular unions, she argues, but they should not participate in supporting an outdated government preference for couples. Hunt is a feminist theologian and the cofounder and codirector of the Women's Alliance for Theology, Ethics and Ritual (WATER).

As you read, consider the following questions:

1. As she explains in the viewpoint, who makes up the author's family?

Mary E. Hunt, "A Marriage Proposal: With Gay Marriage Now On The Agenda, It May Be Time To Consider The Institution Of Marriage Itself," *Conscience*, Summer 2005, pp. 36–38.

2. What is meant by the "white picket fence model" of marriage, as the phrase is used in the viewpoint?
3. What does the author of the viewpoint suggest the clergy do when asked to officiate at weddings?

The best proof that the religious right is in charge in the United States lies in the movement for same-sex marriage. Of course the Right opposes it, but by setting up marriage as the main lesbian/gay/bisexual/transgender/queer (LGBTQ) agenda item, the Right has set itself up to win. This issue, like gays in the military before it, is not necessarily the most important to LGBTQ people ourselves. But the Right's polarizing opposition has made it necessary to struggle for it or lose ground. I make no pretense of solving a difficult problem and I know the injustice of a heterosexist culture. But my modest proposal is intended to reframe the issue.

In fact, what seems to be a huge step forward for lesbian and gay people, will, when achieved, extend the reach of state control over relationships. It will privilege those who are coupled over those who are single or otherwise connected. It will shore up the nuclear family model despite the fact that people live in many other relational constellations. However, if same-sex marriage is prohibited, as the eleven state referenda lost in the last election year [2004] would have it, a significant percentage of the population will continue to lose out on the 1,138 federal rights that marriage conveys. This is a classic "damned if you do, damned if you don't" situation. The Right knows how to frame the issue, a skill I suggest we who have a broader vision learn.

Progressive people, and especially progressive religious people, must do better if relational justice for all—and not just more rights for a few—is to result. In the interest of full disclosure, I live in a long-term committed relationship with a wonderful woman, and we have adopted a daughter. By some lights, we look like the new model of the Catholic Family of the Year. By others, we are the incarnation of evil. By my lights, we are simply three people who deserve all of the rights of citizenship, but no more than my single cousin, my widowed neighbor or my friends who belong to religious congregations. Connecting rights to marriage is, in my view, an outmoded approach to the common good.

Marriage and Privilege

The operative problem is not same-sex marriage, but heterosexual marriage. Hetero-marriage is not a right, but a privilege-granting machine that favors those who are lucky in love by making them even luckier in the business of daily life. I see no reason to extend that privilege to more people, and every reason to curtail it, so as to level the socioeconomic playing field for all. This can only be achieved while building social safeguards for the whole of society, since any protections afforded, especially to women, by hetero-marriage, such as maintenance after divorce, will be lost.

I support the efforts that have resulted in civil unions in Vermont, same-sex marriage in Massachusetts, and the various forays in Oregon, San Francisco, New Paltz, NY, and elsewhere to bring about equality. Far from contradicting myself, I am politically practical enough to realize that without forcing the issue into the courts, it will lie dormant. Moreover, it has been very instructive for the whole country to see that same-sex marriages have not brought about the end of the world, nor have they resulted in the end of heterosexuality as we know it.

If anything, same-sex marriages have fueled the wedding business (catering, photographers, flowers, receptions and gifts galore) and reinforced the notion that "good" gay and lesbian people come in happy twosomes. I favor other economic priorities (like health care for all) and know that many lesbian and gay people are single, between relationships, or quite content to live outside the long arms of the state. But choice is choice and I support it. Nonetheless, my long-term goal is not same-sex marriage. I seek a broader, perhaps more utopian, trajectory toward full citizenship for all with an emphasis on the common good upheld by structures that support individual choices.

Jewish feminist theologian Judith Plaskow and her longtime partner Smith College professor Martha Ackelsberg, who live in Massachusetts, said it best: "In not taking advantage of this new right, however, we can more comfortably advocate for the kind of society in which we would like to live." If those of us who are white, middle or upper middle class and well educated enough to manipulate the legal system do not resist the grinding moves toward social sameness, who will? In addition, African American womanist scholar Irene Monroe has claimed that the move toward same-sex marriage has been a narrow framing of the queer justice agenda, one that leaves aside many of the concerns of African American families including adoption, HIV/AIDS prevention and unemployment. I trust these women's views and prefer them to the [pro-marriage gay writer] Andrew Sullivanesque hand wringing over tying the knot. Interestingly, while gay men have pushed for marriage, the Massachusetts statistics after the first year of same-sex marriage reveal that women are marrying one another at more than twice the rate of men. This is due, no doubt, to the longtime female conditioning to bond and to the economic challenges two women face in what is still—economically speaking—a man's world.

Marriage Is a Business Deal

The debate around same-sex marriage has been very helpful in making transparent several fundamental issues. First, marriage, both hetero and homo, is as much, if not more, a business deal than a romantic or even a religious matter. I say this not to demean or degrade those who choose it, but to explain how the world works so we can make informed choices. For

Relationships Take Many Forms

To have our government define as "legitimate families" only those households with couples in conjugal relationships does a tremendous disservice to the many other ways in which people actually construct their families, kinship networks, households, and relationships. For example, who among us seriously will argue that the following kinds of households are less socially, economically, and spiritually worthy?

- Senior citizens living together, serving as each other's caregivers, partners, and/or constructed families
- Adult children living with and caring for their parents
- Grandparents and other family members raising their children's (and/or a relative's) children
- Committed, loving households in which there is more than one conjugal partner
- Blended families
- Single parent households
- Extended families (especially in particular immigrant populations) living under one roof, whose members care for one another
- Queer couples who decide to jointly create and raise a child with another queer person or couple, in two households
- Close friends and siblings who live together in long-term, committed, non-conjugal relationships, serving as each other's primary support and caregivers

"Beyond Same-Sex Marriage: A New Strategic Vision for All Our Families and Relationships," July 26, 2006. www.beyondmarriage.org.

example, hetero-marriage assures the sharing of Social Security benefits, certain pension survivor's rights and the option to file joint income taxes when doing so will be favorable. Of course, one need not be heterosexual to marry as it is. The late Andrea Dworkin, a lesbian feminist activist who was a critic of marriage, married her longtime companion John Stoltenberg, a gay man. Their motives are none of my business, but I suspect business entered into the decision since access to a partner's insurance coverage, for example, is easier for married people.

It is simply ethically intuitive to extend such privileges to same-sex couples who, by marrying, take on the various responsibilities that heterosexual couples claim justify their privilege. But what remains to be explained is why being coupled, especially without children, should result in any economic advantage. Rather, it seems fair that everyone should be able to designate survivors for purposes of inheritance, or no one should; everyone ought to be able to choose with whom they will jointly file taxes, or no one should. Thousands of same-sex couples married in Massachusetts are finding out as they file their first income taxes as married couples that the "full faith and credit" is not an easy constitutional mandate to fulfill. Married in their state's eyes, they have to file their federal returns as single people.

The court challenges in this regard promise to be many and lengthy as same-sex marriage plays out first in the states and eventually at the federal level. I am persuaded, along with Sue Hyde of the National Gay and Lesbian Task Force that "same-sex marriage is a reality; it's here to stay and it will eventually become the law of the land." My concern is whether marriage is actually what we want, the short-term justice goal it represents notwithstanding.

Marriage Supports a Fiction

The more I examine marriage, the more obvious it becomes that the laws are written to favor a certain two-by-two lifestyle that is simply a fiction. A divorce rate above 40 percent and the growing number of longtime single people in our society suggest that for many people marriage is at best a temporary state of affairs. It would seem to make more sense to draw the legal lines vis-à-vis those who have children or even those who care for elders, privileging them because they have taken on the care of those who cannot care for themselves. But doing so in the case of children would reinforce the notion that children "belong" to their parents, rather than being the responsibility of society as a whole; it would reinforce that elder care is family- rather than society-based.

A second problem with marriage, delicate to handle without being accused of promoting promiscuity, is one raised by LGBTQ Canadians who have the right to marry but do not seem to be exercising it in the same proportions as their U.S. counterparts. Is hetero-marriage, with its presumption of sexual exclusivity, really what lesbian and gay people want? Do we intend to perpetuate what one Canadian referred to as the "white picket fence model," the fiction that happiness and relational goodness only come in matched pairs?

I admit to being on the conventional side here, and so, fortunately for me, is my partner. But I see no good reason to legislate such morality when other people find different models that suit their mutual tastes. It is hard to know the players without a scorecard, but polyamory is increasingly acceptable in some circles. Celibacy is also an option that, in my view, deserves equal treatment under the law. Discussion of same-sex marriage lays bare how stiflingly rigid we are when it comes to encouraging relational diversity. Same-sex divorces will make the shortcomings of marriage even more obvious, with lawyers waiting happily in the wings to profit from our losses. I see no reason to reinforce such a dysfunctional model by insisting on admitting more people to it, though I understand that everyone should have the right to be wrong.

A third major flaw in the marriage model is the relationship between religion and the state that is a major part of the same-sex marriage debate. One of the reasons given to prohibit same-sex marriages is that many ministers, rabbis, imams and other religious professionals who now act on behalf of the state could be forced to do so against their religious principles if same-sex marriage becomes an option. While I doubt any court would so order, what I hope will result from this discussion is a wholesale rethinking of the role of religious professionals in the state's business.

The Role of the Clergy

It is not clear to me why clergy people handle the legal aspects of marriage at all, signing off as official representatives of the state. It would seem that judges, justices of the peace and other duly elected or appointed government officials should do so, leaving religious professionals to tend to the spiritual dimensions of relationships for those who wish to avail themselves of such services. This is done in many countries as a routine matter. Note that Prince Charles and Camilla Parker Bowles married first in a civil ceremony (the real thing, that Queen Elizabeth took a pass on) and then had a religious blessing (which the queen attended since it, like the reception, had no legal weight). I remain mystified as to why clergy in the United States willingly work for the state without pay or pension.

Many progressive religious people, including me, have been supportive of the same-sex marriage movement. I believe that we need to continue that public support, including risking ecclesial and/or civil disobedience in doing so. But at the same time, and without risk of contradiction, I think we need to raise the kinds of issues I am flagging here so as to avoid being co-opted by the Religious Right one more time.

We need to admit that many of our religious traditions have not strayed far from their roots when it comes to marriage as a commodity exchange. We, as their current leaders, need to put a wholesale re-examination of marriage on the agenda, leaving aside the same-sex distraction in order to think anew about how we envision a just society.

Religious leaders would do everyone a favor by breaking out of the moral mold and talking frankly about what we know to be the many and varied ways good people live their relational lives. We need to bring the moral energies of religion to the realities of contemporary social life. This does not mean that we abdicate ethics, but that we listen hard and speak honestly about the fact that two-by-two is not the only, and for some not the best, way to live. It is because religions put such a priority on those who are vulnerable or marginalized, like the young, the old and the infirm, that religious leaders can dare to entertain relational models other than marriage without risking the loss of what marriage now purports to protect. Someone has to start the conversation.

Religious leaders, especially licensed clergy, will need to lead the way in separating religion and the state by refusing to function on the state's behalf at weddings. When asked to officiate, I suggest that clergy think twice, steering people to the state for the legal part and of course welcoming all who wish a religious service of blessing on their partnerships, their extended families, or their solitary splendor. That action alone would move this question forward by light years.

Let the Religious Right struggle with these challenges and perhaps same-sex couples can marry, or not, in peace.

Viewpoint 7

> *"Children need both men and women as role models."*

Same-Sex Couples Pose a Threat to Children in Their Care

"An Adoptive Father"

The following viewpoint was originally published as a letter to the editor of Commonweal: A Review of Public Affairs, Religion, Literature and the Arts. *The author, who signs simply as "An Adoptive Father," argues that same-sex couples should not adopt children. These children, he contends, are already suffering from emotional loss and confusion, and even with the nurturing of a mother and a father they can have difficulty healing. While adopting children is undoubtedly rewarding for same-sex couples, he concludes, it is not in the best interest of the children.*

As you read, consider the following questions:

1. Whose viewpoint is rarely considered when people discuss adoption by same-sex couples, according to the author?

"An Adoptive Father", "Gay Adoption: Unprecedented Experiment," *Commonweal*, vol. 134, September 14, 2007, pp. 4, 34.

2. As reported in the viewpoint, when did the author's adopted daughter contact her adoption agency to search for her birth mother?
3. Why, according to the viewpoint, are gay male couples particularly ill-suited to raise children?

The discussion of homosexuality in your June 15 issue by Eve Tushnet and Luke Timothy Johnson ("Homosexuality & Scripture") has prompted me to say a word on gay adoption. My wife and I have a "natural" child and an adopted child. We both feel deeply that the traumas of adoption—of lost or uncertain identity, of troubled relations with adoptive parents, as experienced at one or another time by virtually all adopted children, and as witnessed and experienced by adoptive parents too—are so grave and disruptive (and in some cases disabling for the child) that to add to this an arbitrary imposition of monosexual parentage is a very grave step, involving an enormous responsibility for the life of another human who has no say in the matter.

The issue is nearly always discussed simply from the viewpoint of the prospective parents. Rarely considered is the situation of the child who will bear the consequences. Objections are often dismissed with the argument that a loving home is surely better than an orphanage. No doubt it is, but it is my impression that most gay adoptions in the United States and in other advanced countries involve children who are deliberately conceived for adoption, with the help of a friend, a commercial sperm bank, or a young woman willing to bear the child, sometimes for a price—all of which dreadfully complicates the identity quest, as a number of recent personal accounts attest. (These children are not being rescued from Ceausescu-era Romanian orphanages.)

The question of origin and identity usually arises for an adopted child as he or she passes through late adolescence. In the case of our own child, raised in a "normal" middle-class

Gay Parenting in Texas

There are more gay couples with children in the South than in any other region. Texas in particular has been at the forefront of the gay parenting boom: According to a study of the 2000 census by the Urban Institute, a nonpartisan think tank, homosexual couples in Texas are more likely to have children than those in almost any other state. Nationally, about one in four gay couples has children; in Texas, the figure is closer to one in three. San Antonio, surprisingly, has emerged as an unlikely gay parenting mecca, with the nation's highest percentage of gay households with children. The reason for this is unclear, though it may have something to do with the city's sizable number of Catholics, like Nagle and Pinkham. A good number of these children are being adopted following foster care placements through CPS [Child Protective Services] though the agency can't say for certain how many. (Foster care is a temporary arrangement supervised by the state; adoption is a legal proceeding granting permanent custody.)

Nate Blakeslee, "Family Values," Texas Monthly, *vol. 35, no. 3, March 2007, pp. 142–45, 284–92, 298.*

professional family free of crises, with a loving and protective older brother as well as loving parents, our daughter came close to being lost to us, and to herself, during adolescence, when, as she told me recently: "I hated you even while I loved you. Who were you to do this to me? Where was my mother? Why had she abandoned me?"

She survived, as did we, and is now married with three young children of her own. But when each of her two daughters was born, she was thrown into a crisis of rejection and confusion for which she sought psychiatric counseling. At thirty-eight, after the birth of her youngest daughter, she approached her adoption agency to try to find her birth mother—so as to find closure, she said, even though she recognized that the search might fail, or worse. Then as the emotions provoked by her own daughter's birth eased—when she had again asked, how could my "real" mother have abandoned me, given me away?—she gave up the search, but the question stays with her.

An Unprecedented Experiment

Gay adoption is a privileged society's historically and socially unprecedented experiment with helpless lives, an experiment justified as affording "equality" for homosexuals. But equality is not equivalence. To impose on an infant a lifetime experience not only of the crisis of normal adoption but also of the absence of normal heterosexual psychological (and even physiological) parental modeling and influence is to risk inflicting a crippling wound on the victim of this experiment in order to provide adult homosexuals with the gratification of love. This gratification is real, of course, but for the child it means the artificial circumstances and social disadvantage of a simulacrum of heterosexual marriage.

This seems particularly grave in the case of male homosexual alliances. I believe that competent authority amply supports the common-sense conclusion that a man is not physiologically or emotionally equipped to be a mother. A man does not nurture as a woman nurtures, nor can a man substitute for a woman as a model for serious and balanced sexual maturation of the child. Children need both men and women as role models. I am reminded of the crisis of clerical pedophilia—a matter that is not, alas, wholly irrelevant to the adoption issue—in which church authorities willfully ignored the obvious for reasons of scandal-avoidance, priestly solidarity, convenience, cowardice, etc., until a disaster exploded in their faces. A generation from now, I am convinced, equivalent reproaches will be expressed with respect to the children made part of the experiment in gay adoption, which enjoys the endorsement of many well-meaning people today, including a significant segment of the Christian community. Of course, there are loving homosexual couples who are committed to responsible parenthood. But men and women have to take responsibility for what they are, and for the consequences of what they do, even when they do it with love.

Because the editors know my address and identity, I hope that for the sake of my adopted daughter and grandchildren's privacy I may be allowed to remain anonymous.

VIEWPOINT 8

> *"Lesbian co-mothers seem to be more involved in the lives of their children than are heterosexual fathers."*

Many Same-Sex Couples Make Good Parents

William Meezan and Jonathan Rauch

In the following viewpoint, William Meezan and Jonathan Rauch examine the results of several psychological studies, and conclude that there is no scientific evidence that being raised by gay or lesbian parents is harmful to children. Having gay or lesbian parents does not confuse children about their own identities, they argue, nor does it affect their emotional development. Meezan is dean of the College of Social Work at the Ohio State University. Raunch is a journalist who writes about U.S. government public policy in general, and specifically, in its relation to homosexuals.

As you read, consider the following questions:

1. According to the viewpoint, how might conservatives and liberals interpret the attitudes of young women raised in lesbian-headed families differently?

2. What is the only negative suggestion raised by studies of the emotional development of children of same-sex parents, as reported in the viewpoint?
3. How many children have been involved in studies of families with same-sex parents, according to the viewpoint?

The American Psychological Association concluded in its July 2004 "Resolution on Sexual Orientation, Parents, and Children,"

> There is no scientific basis for concluding that lesbian mothers or gay fathers are unfit parents on the basis of their sexual orientation. . . . On the contrary, results of research suggest that lesbian and gay parents are as likely as heterosexual parents to provide supportive and healthy environments for their children. . . . Overall results of research suggest that the development, adjustment, and well-being of children with lesbian and gay parents do not differ markedly from that of children with heterosexual parents.

Our own review of the evidence is consistent with that characterization. Specifically, the research supports four conclusions.

First, lesbian mothers, and gay fathers (about whom less is known), are much like other parents. Where differences are found, they sometimes favor same-sex parents. For instance, although one study finds that heterosexual fathers had greater emotional involvement with their children than did lesbian co-mothers, others find either no difference or that lesbian co-mothers seem to be more involved in the lives of their children than are heterosexual fathers.

Second, there is no evidence that children of lesbian and gay parents are confused about their gender identity, either in childhood or adulthood, or that they are more likely to be homosexual. Evidence on gender behavior (as opposed to identification) is mixed; some studies find no differences, whereas others find that girls raised by lesbians may be more "masculine" in play and aspirations and that boys of lesbian parents are less aggressive. Finally, some interesting differences have been noted in sexual behavior and attitudes (as opposed to orientation). Some studies report that children, particularly daughters, of lesbian parents adopt more accepting and open attitudes toward various sexual identities and are more willing to question their own sexuality. Others report that young women raised in lesbian-headed families are more likely to have homosexual friends and to disclose that they have had or would consider having same-sex sexual relationships. (Just how to view such differences in behavior and attitude is a matter of disagreement. Where conservatives may see lax or immoral sexual standards, liberals may see commendably open-minded attitudes.)

Children and Emotional Well-Being

Third, in general, children raised in same-sex environments show no differences in cognitive abilities, behavior, general emotional development, or such specific areas of emotional development as self-esteem, depression, or anxiety. In the few cases where differences in emotional development are found, they tend to favor children raised in lesbian families. For example, one study reports that preschool children of lesbian mothers tend to be less aggressive, bossy, and domineering than children of heterosexual mothers. Another finds more psychiatric difficulties and a greater number of psychiatric referrals among children of heterosexual parents. The only negative suggestion to have been uncovered about the emotional development of children of same-sex parents is a fear on the part of the children—which seems to dissipate during adolescence when sexual orientation is first expressed—that they might be homosexual.

Finally, many gay and lesbian parents worry about their children being teased, and children often expend emotional

Scientific Research Shows That Children of Gay Parents Are Just as Healthy and Well-Adjusted as Other Children

Until the 1970s, there was virtually no scientific research on gay parents or their children because there were not very many openly gay parents to study. Until then, lesbians and gay men raising children generally were not open about their sexual orientation for reasonable fear of losing custody of their children or other forms of discrimination. It wasn't until the gay liberation movement was well underway that lesbian mothers and gay fathers began to come out in significant numbers, providing subjects to study. And the 1980s marked the beginning of the "lesbian baby boom," a rise in lesbian couples planning families together through adoption or assisted reproductive technology. More and more gay male couples are also choosing to become parents.

With the appearance of openly gay and lesbian parents in the last quarter century, and in significant numbers in the past 20 years, scientists have had the opportunity to study these families, evaluating the parenting abilities of lesbian and gay parents and how well their children are developing. There is now a well-developed body of scientific research on lesbian and gay parents and their children in scholarly journals. The academic literature includes more than two dozen studies that have evaluated several hundred parents and children. The studies found, without exception, that gay people are just as capable parents and that children raised by lesbians and gay men are just as healthy and well-adjusted as other children.

Leslie Cooper and Paul Cates, Too High a Price: The Case Against Restricting Gay Parenting. *New York: American Civil Liberties Foundation, 2006.*

energy hiding or otherwise controlling information about their parents, mainly to avoid ridicule. The evidence is mixed, however, on whether the children have heightened difficulty with peers, with more studies finding no particular problems.

Controversial Research

The significance of this body of evidence is a matter of contention, to say the least. Steven Nock, a prominent scholar reviewing the literature in 2001 as an expert witness in a Canadian court case, found it so flawed methodologically that the "only acceptable conclusion at this point is that the literature on this topic does not constitute a solid body of scientific evidence," and that "all of the articles I reviewed contained at least one fatal flaw of design or execution. . . . Not a single one was conducted according to generally accepted standards of scientific research." Two equally prominent scholars, Judith Stacey and Timothy Biblarz, vigorously disputed the point: "He is simply wrong to say that all of the studies published to date are virtually worthless and unscientific. . . . If the Court were to accept Professor Nock's primary criticisms of these studies, it would have to dismiss virtually the entire discipline of psychology."

We believe that both sides of that argument are right, at least partially. The evidence provides a great deal of information about the particular families and children studied, and the children now number more than a thousand. They are doing about as well as children normally do. What the evidence does not provide, because of the methodological difficulties we outlined, is much knowledge about whether those studied are typical or atypical of the general population of children raised by gay and lesbian couples. We do not know how the *normative* child in a same-sex family compares with other children. To make the same point a little differently, those who say the evidence shows that many same-sex parents do an excellent job of parenting are right. Those who say the evidence falls short of showing that same-sex parenting is equivalent to opposite-sex parenting (or better, or worse) are also right.

Periodical Bibliography

The following articles have been selected to supplement the diverse views presented in this chapter.

Nate Blakeslee	"Family Values," *Texas Monthly*, March 2007.
Andrew Bolt	"Kids Pay for Gay Marriage," *Sunday Mail (Australia)*, June 18, 2006.
Brian Callaway	"A Civil War over Civil Unions?" *Morning Call (Allentown, PA)*, February 19, 2007.
Nadine Chaffee	"One Son's Choice: Love or Country?" *Newsweek*, February 5, 2007.
Catherine Deveny	"Gay Marriage? Sure, but Why Would Anyone Want to?" *The Age (Melbourne, Australia)*, February 28, 2007.
Rita Giordano	"Smiles and Vows for Civil Unions," *Philadelphia Inquirer*, February 23, 2007.
Murray Hausknecht	"Gay Marriage: The Third Option," *Dissent*, Spring 2007.
John Heard	"Leave Wedded Bliss to Those Who Can Make Babies," *Australian*, March 19, 2007.
Gregory M. Herek	"Legal Recognition of Same-Sex Relationships in the United States: A Social Science Perspective," *American Psychologist*, September 2006.
Stanley Kurtz	"Here Come the Brides: Plural Marriage Is Waiting in the Wings," *Weekly Standard*, December 26, 2005.
Jay F. Marks	"Same-Sex Adoption Law Struck," *Daily Oklahoman*, May 20, 2006.
Debra Rosenberg and Karen Breslau	"The Wedding March," *Newsweek*, August 7, 2006.
Bill Salisbury	"Voters Oppose Gay Marriage Amendment," *St. Paul Pioneer Press*, September 28, 2006.

Chapter 4

What Should Schools Teach About Homosexuality?

Chapter Preface

On January 1, 2008, a new law took effect in California. The law, called the California Student Civil Rights Act, S.B.777, prohibits public schools from engaging in discrimination based on religion, race, disability, and gender. Controversially, the law also forbids discrimination based on sexual orientation. The law requires that no instructional materials may present negative attitudes toward any people because of their gender or sexual orientation, and that no student may be excluded from school-sponsored activities based on gender or sexual orientation.

In the eyes of many, the bill was a sign of real progress. For too long, they said, GLBT (gay, lesbian, bisexual, or transgendered) students had been treated badly at school. The National Education Association reported in 2006 that "more than 91 percent of GLBT students say they hear homophobic slurs or expressions frequently . . . and more than 64 percent of GLBT students say they feel unsafe at school because of their sexual orientation." Public schools are meant to serve all citizens, they argued, including gay and lesbian students and parents, and all students have a right to feel safe. In addition, they argued, a curriculum that ignores the existence of gay men and lesbians is incomplete. Gay men and lesbians do exist, and have been important contributors to history, science, and the arts; the new law, in this view, simply encourages an acknowledgement of that fact.

But from the time the bill was introduced, parent groups and religious organizations worked actively to stop what they saw as a serious threat to school children, posed by the "homosexual agenda." California parent Karen England commented, "S.B.777 is designed to transform our public schools into institutions that disregard all notions of the traditional family unit. This reverse discrimination is an outright attack on the religious and moral beliefs of California citizens." Opponents of the bill feared that it could have wide-ranging repercussions: That competitions for prom kings and queens would be forbidden because they demonstrate bias; that teachers would be sued for saying common phrases like "Mom and Dad"; that even young children would be encouraged to explore their sexual orientation; and that students would be prohibited from expressing their families' negative views about homosexuality.

People often say that going to school is preparation for the "real world," but there seems to be no real consensus about what that means. Should school teach students a set of facts, or a set of skills they can draw on later to process facts? Should schools teach students what is right and wrong, or how to develop their own beliefs? Should schools teach children about the world as it is, or as we wish it to be? And, if controversial realities are to be discussed in school, what is the appropriate age for students to participate in these discussions? These broad questions have led parents to challenge the way schools present information and ideas about a range of topics, including religion, poverty, crime, war, drugs, violence—and sexual orientation.

Is there a place for sexual orientation in a school curriculum? Many parents and teachers say no. Sexual orientation is a controversial subject, they say, and it should be up to individual families to teach their values to their own children. Others say yes, a curriculum should reflect the full range of human experience. In this chapter, teachers, parents, and journalists debate how—and whether—children should develop an awareness of sexual orientation.

VIEWPOINT 1

"Over 80 percent of teens consider human sexuality and sexual relationships equally or more important than other subjects taught in school."

Children Should Be Taught in School to Understand Homosexuality

Arthur Lipkin

In the following viewpoint, Arthur Lipkin answers some of the most commonly asked questions in regard to including the topic of homosexuality in the elementary and secondary school classroom. He contends that avoiding mentioning gay men and women in subjects such as literature or history denies the existence and important contributions of a segment of the population. Including this material in school, he argues, gives children a structured way to discuss sexuality away from the warping influences of popular culture. Lipkin is a research associate in Human Development and Psychology at the Harvard Graduate School of Education and the author of Beyond Diversity Day *(2004), from which this viewpoint was taken.*

Arthur Lipkin, *Beyond Diversity Day: A Q & A on Gay and Lesbian Issues in Schools*. Lanham, MD: Rowman & Littlefield Publishers, Inc., 2004.

As you read, consider the following questions:

1. What happened to mathematician Alan Turing toward the end of his life, as reported in the viewpoint?
2. What current events topics involving sexual orientation would be appropriate for discussions in school, according to the viewpoint?
3. How could introducing gay content enrich English as a second language classes, according to the viewpoint?

Why should the topic of homosexuality be included in the curriculum?

The humanistic reason for teaching students about homosexuality is to increase understanding of diversity, to lessen antigay bigotry, and to foster the healthy development of all youth. But there are other pedagogically sound reasons as well. Chief among them is that issues of sexuality—both its norms and its variations—rivet adolescents. Over 80 percent of teens consider human sexuality and sexual relationships equally or more important than other subjects taught in school. Anyone concerned about teaching to students' interests should welcome the inclusion of accurate unsensationalized lessons on all aspects of sexuality. They provide a necessary balance to the entertainment media's exploitation of sex to sell products.

However it arises, sexual curiosity is an important part of an adolescent's intellectual and emotional development. Even younger children who are not ready for detailed explanations would benefit from the teachable moments that our sexualized popular culture provides.

Finally, a complete and honest curriculum is more alive and powerful than a censored one. Students are put off by instruction that ignores the world they live in. But do not assume that a curriculum has to be trendy or shallow to be appealing. Genuine nuanced lessons can encourage students to think critically and deeply about their own experiences and the lives of others. . . .

Is this not more propaganda than education?

Many conservatives claim that blocking gay content in education would maintain schools as "sexuality-free" or neutral spaces. They are being disingenuous. Classrooms and school lessons have always been both sexualized and heterosexist. Most students, at least from preadolescence, are active players in the cultural dramas of sex and gender, egged on by sex-saturated mass media. School curricula do their part in reinforcing a prescribed heterosexual norm in arguably every subject area. At the same time heterosexist notions and homophobic behaviors are rarely challenged in schools. The reform recommendations in this book are aimed at correcting these existing problems of sexuality bias and bigotry. Doing nothing is not neutral.

Which academic disciplines most often incorporate gay content?

Homosexuality, if it is brought up at all, is discussed most commonly in the health class, frequently in connection with HIV/AIDS. Even so, the amount of HIV/AIDS education deemed "highly sensitive" to the needs of glbt [gay, lesbian, bisexual, and transgendered] youth is miniscule. Prevention is still taught with a heterosexual slant. Safer sex information for all should be part of a comprehensive health curriculum, but when students hear about glbt people *only* in this context, they could conclude that homosexuality is mainly about pathology. That is not the way to reduce homophobia or help glbt students develop a positive identity.

Moreover, confining homosexuality to health curricula reduces gays and lesbians to the physical domain. The study of straight sexuality in the health class is at least balanced by a more holistic study of male-female relationships in history, literature, and other subjects.

Even when the goal is sex education, the curriculum must be about more than plumbing. To be credible and effective, it must address pleasure, spirituality, and power in every kind of sexual relationship. . . .

What areas in social studies present opportunities for inclusion?

History, political science, sociology, anthropology, and psychology are natural places for gay and lesbian curricula. Topics might include:

- how same-gender sexuality has been understood and judged in different cultures and periods;
- the evolution of modern Western glbt identities;
- important "homosexual" people in history;
- current gay issues, including civil rights, medicine, activism, and politics.

Although lists of prominent glbt historical figures make a nice display, they don't become a curriculum until the "poster people" are studied. For instance, students could simply be told that gay mathematician Alan Turing helped break the Nazi war codes and start the computer industry, but the *indispensable* human rights lesson lies in the study of his arrest for homosexual activity, his forced hormone therapy, and his suicide. To that end, they might read or see the play/video *Breaking the Code*, based on Turing's life. As another example, they could examine why what would later be called "gay liberation" was an integral part of Emma Goldman's radical agenda in the 1920s.

The documentary film *Out of the Past* documents the historical progression of homosexuality from sin to sickness to community through the lives of Michael Wigglesworth, Sarah Orne Jewett, and Barbara Gittings. Bayard Rustin, another of the film's subjects, personifies the convergence of multiple identities in a social justice warrior. A gay, African American leftist who triumphed over sexual, racial, and political obstacles, Rustin organized the 1964 March on Washington for Civil Rights.

The list of figures inviting study is easily expanded to: T. E. Lawrence, Dag Hammerskjold, Margaret Fuller, Susan B. Anthony, Katharine Lee Bates (lyricist of "America the Beautiful"), Irish patriot Sir Roger Casement, Sweden's Queen Christina, leaders in medicine and public health like Sara Josephine Baker, domestic partners Ethel Collins Dunham and Martha May Eliot, and many others.

Aren't these lists of famous homosexuals far-fetched?

The sexuality of historical figures, especially of the pre-twentieth century, is sometimes hard to categorize. As much as gay people, like other minorities, want to take pride in the lives of great forebears, teachers need to be as accurate as they can be.

For example, although he shared a bed with another man for three years, Abraham Lincoln was less likely gay than was James Buchanan, whose sexuality was openly questioned during his presidency. Both men may exemplify nineteenth-century intimate and effusive male bonding more than homosexuality. Good student research on such questions is more important than the conclusive verdicts.

How can modern gay history be included?

U.S. history and sociology classes could study gay liberation in comparison to other civil rights' struggles. One might begin with the 1969 Stonewall Riots in New York, the raucous eruption of drag queens and street youth that has been called the spark of the modern gay movement. It offers colorful firsthand accounts that engage students. It can also provide an entry point to a more complete history, including its antecedents. An overview of same-gender sexuality from the colonial period through the pre-Stonewall years could focus on urbanization, the ascendancy of science, the impact of the world wars, and Nazi victimization.

Creating an Inclusive Environment for School Athletes

Why is it especially important for physical educators and coaches to create a safe and inclusive environment? LGBT [lesbian, gay, bisexual, and transgendered] students and athletes often claim that physical education classes and athletic environments are where they feel least safe and least supported. Environments that create this perception are often referred to as homophobic. Homophobia is defined as an irrational fear of lesbians and gay men. This definition implies that the fear is of an unknown origin and that there is little that can be done to influence it. We purposefully choose to use the term "homonegative," even though "homophobia" is the more recognized term. We believe that the fear is not irrational, but that it is learned from parents and peers, and teachers and coaches, as well as from the environment in which individuals interact daily. If homonegativism is learned, then it can be unlearned or, better yet, never learned. If physical activity and sport environments are perceived as homonegative, we can and need to actively work to change that climate so that it will not teach or reinforce discrimination.

Heather Barber and Vikki Krane, JOPERD—
The Journal of Physical Education, Recreation & Dance,
September 2007, vol. 78, no. 7, p. 6.

Compelling topics in the thirty years after Stonewall include: the gay movement's shift from sexual freedom to civil rights, de-listing homosexuality as a mental illness, the role and image of women and transgender people in the liberation struggle, and the effect of HIV/AIDS on the glbt community and its politics. Moreover, the growing literature on regional

U.S. history (e.g., George Chauncey's *Gay New York*, James T. Sears's *Lonely Hunters: An Oral History of Lesbian and Gay Southern Life 1948–1968*, and the History Project's *Improper Bostonians*) can bring gay history literally home to students. Lastly, the ongoing public discourse on gay marriage and gays in the military, Boy Scouts, and Big Brothers are appropriate to current events discussions and debates. . . .

What can be done in language arts and literature?

Glbt life is treated in fiction and biography, prose and poetry. Students can study the details of such literature in which homosexuality is explicit or clearly implied. They could also investigate other work by glbt writers to see how their sexualities might have influenced their perspective, that is, to see whether writing by a homosexual author can still be considered gay writing even when it has no apparent gay content.

Some glbt writers like [Walt] Whitman, [Andre] Gide, [Henry] James, [Lorraine] Hansberry, and [James] Baldwin are already part of school syllabi. Others whose sexualities are uncertain or harder to classify also make for interesting analysis, such as [Christopher] Marlowe, [Johann Wolfgang von] Goethe, [Lord] Byron, [Emily] Dickinson, [Gerard Manley] Hopkins, and [Langston] Hughes.

World and immigrant literature can enhance students' appreciation of the international scope of "homosexualities." Likewise, gay content in English as a second language and bilingual materials creates opportunities to broach the issue of sexual diversity with students from other cultures.

What is the point of raising an author's sexuality when it is ambiguous or irrelevant?

Sexuality, like gender or race, is often an important factor in a writer's life and hence an influence on his or her work. It is crucial to understanding many heterosexual authors—and not just the salient ones like [Anaïs] Nin or [Ernest] Hemingway. Yet when teachers want to explore homosexuality (apparent or speculative), they often encounter a double standard concerning its relevance and appropriateness.

Asking whether particular authors experienced same-gender attractions, what these feelings may have signified to them, and how both are reflected in their work can be illuminating. For example, Thoreau's possible homosexuality helps us analyze the romanticism of his poem "Sympathy" ("Lately, alas, I knew a gentle boy") and provides a fascinating perspective on *Walden*.

There is much to mine as well in Langston Hughes's eleven-line poem, "Café: 3 a.m.," about undercover police officers arresting "fairies" in the 1950s. Besides raising the provocative issue of Hughes's own sexuality, the poem can serve as an introduction to other Harlem Renaissance figures who were openly gay and lesbian, like Bessie Smith, Gladys Bentley, Ma Rainey, Countee Cullen, Bruce Nugent, and Wallace Thurman.

Many have studied Willa Cather's "Paul's Case" without reference to the sexuality of either the title character or the author. No one can really understand that short story without a gay lens. Although we don't have to know every detail about Cather's women companions, the story resonates quite differently if we know about Cather's early condemnation of Oscar Wilde and her own masquerade—as a man!

Billy Budd, the "Handsome Sailor," can be read as a tale of repressed homoerotic desire. Moreover, Ishmael and Queequeg's relationship in *Moby Dick* is cast in a new light when students learn about Melville's views of sexuality in the South Seas islands and his passionate relationship with Hawthorne.

Homosexual possibilities arise in Shakespeare, too. Although critics may challenge such interpretations, they would be hard pressed to censor the "classics."

Viewpoint 2

"Parents want the assurance that . . . their children . . . will learn the fundamentals of reading, writing, and arithmetic—not social indoctrination regarding alternative sexual lifestyles."

Schools Should Not Address Homosexuality

Bob Unruh

In the following viewpoint, Bob Unruh addresses California Senate Bill 777, a 2007 law that gave schools guidelines for including information about homosexuality. Unruh contends that this law is part of a plan by the homosexual lobby to indoctrinate students, leading them to accept homosexuality as normal. Most parents, he argues, do not want sexuality to be discussed at school, and many will remove their children from public school rather than expose them to activist propaganda. Unruh is a news editor for WorldNetDaily.com, an independent news company that promotes freedom, self-government, and good character.

As you read, consider the following questions:

1. What did the Save Our Kids project hope to accomplish by collecting signatures, according to the viewpoint?

Bob Unruh, "Stripped Bare: 'Gay' School Plot Unveiled," December 11, 2007. www.worldnetdaily.com. Reproduced by permission.

2. According to Karen England of Save Our Kids, why do discussions of controversial lifestyles not belong in the classroom?
3. How has the proposed curriculum affected public school and home school enrollments, as reported in the viewpoint?

On the heels of Gov. Arnold Schwarzenegger's signature on S.B. [California Senate Bill] 777, which opponents describe as a homosexual indoctrination plan for education districts, a pro-homosexual lobbying organization in California has launched its campaign to infuse a "gay" influence into public school curricula.

The Gay Straight Alliance [GSA] recently forwarded an e-mail to its California chapters with information on how to make sure homosexuality is taught in the state's schools and warned that having students and parents simply "tolerate" homosexuality is not enough

"In many schools, learning about LGBTQ [lesbian, gay, bisexual, transgendered, queer] issues takes the form of very necessary tolerance education where students are educated about the importance of not discriminating against each other," according to GSA documents. "Tolerance education is an important first step, but we need to push further."

"Infuse LGBTQ curriculum into history, social science, and literature classes," is the organization's plan.

Promoting the Homosexual Lifestyle

Karen England, a spokeswoman for Capital Resource Institute who publicized the GSA campaign and is a primary organizer behind the Save Our Kids plan to put the issue before voters and ask them to reject it, said this is exactly what she expected of those who wish to promote the homosexual lifestyle.

"The homosexual lobby is active and ambitious. They already have GSA units in many California schools that will oversee the implementation of S.B.777," England said. "As evidenced in the GSA e-mail, their agenda is inclusion in school instruction and activities, regardless of their public assertions of 'streamlining' anti-discrimination policies in the law."

She said the GSA "guide" to be used tells students "that insisting on LGBTQ history in school instruction 'helps to create schools where students feel safer and more supported.'"

"Utilizing the slogan 'Let's Set the Record Straight: History Isn't', students are given several action steps to take in accomplishing their 'curriculum campaign' goal. These include monitoring classroom instruction to see if LGBTQ individuals are discussed or 'made invisible'; taking over class to present LGBTQ history lessons and contacting textbook companies to change curriculum," England noted.

She said no child should be subjected to discrimination, "but incorporating discussions of an instruction about controversial lifestyles in the classroom does not accomplish this goal. Instead, it undermines parental authority over children's moral upbringing."

The documentation promotes a classroom discussion of Sylvia Rivera, a "Latina transwoman," and suggests, "It's time to take action!"

"Are your teachers teaching about the historical achievements of LGBTQ individuals? Are these issues included in your textbooks? . . ." the organization wrote. "Take over class! . . . Lead a discussion about LGBTQ history or present a lesson of your own."

England said with the pending implementation of S.B.777, soon such messages will come not from independent advocacy groups such as GSA, but from the state's superintendent of Public Instruction, Jack O'Connell.

"That will be the mandate if our referendum isn't successful," she told WND [WorldNetDaily.com]. "It won't be just some San Francisco school. It will be the San Francisco curriculum and values forced on school districts in California."

Controversial Issues Do Not Belong in the Classroom

She called the agenda "highly offensive" to most Californians, in fact, "most Americans."

"Religious background or not, you don't want these controversial issues discussed in a classroom," she said.

She said the Save Our Kids campaign is on track, with more than enough petitions in circulation to collect the signatures needed to present the plan to voters.

But she said petition signature collectors now need to be getting the pages of signatures back to the campaign office to be processed and submitted to the state.

She described the citizen response so far as incredible.

"We have people who are saying, 'Not with my kids, not with my grandkids,'" she said. "Citizens who have never done anything [politically] are setting up tables outside of grocery stores."

The homosexual promotions suggested a "gay/lesbian teacher as role model," promoted the life stories of celebrity homosexuals, and suggests study of *The Kinsey Report*, which in 1948 explored "same-sex sexual behavior."

It also advocates teaching "the truth about historical figures."

"We will never know how he (Abraham Lincoln) might identify his own sexual orientation if he were alive today . . ." the group states. "It is good for young people of all sexual orientations and gender identities to know that some of the legends in their history books were more complex than those books make them seem."

Citizens Must Resist Indoctrination

Brad Dacus, president of Pacific Justice Institute, said, "It is within our reach to defeat S.B.777—the most blatant attempt yet to mandate pro-homosexual and transgender propaganda

The Dangers of "Tolerance Education"

Picture a room packed with five-year-olds sitting cross-legged on the floor. God made them vulnerable for a time to everything adults tell them. Indeed, they can be made to believe that reindeer fly and Santa Claus climbs down the chimneys of every house in the world in a single night. Because of this uncritical acceptance of what they are taught, teachers and administrators have enormous power either to inspire and elevate their developing little minds, or to inculcate within them all manner of base, immoral and harmful ideas. I know this as a former teacher. I always considered my responsibility to the children and their parents to be a sacred trust that demanded the highest degree of integrity. I'm convinced that the vast majority of educators today identify with that high sense of calling. They are dedicated to their profession and are doing a marvelous job under what are often very difficult circumstances. But there are others, including a majority in the California legislature, who would seize the opportunity for manipulation of children and abuse it for political gain. If they are allowed to do so for thirteen formative years of a child's life, he or she will never fully recover from it. Nor will the society they ultimately inherit.

James C. Dobson, "Education Turned Perversion," Focus on the Family Newsletter, *June 2006. www.focusonthefamily.com.*

in schools. We urge all friends of liberty to send CRFI [Capitol Resource Family Impact] their completed petitions as soon as possible."

WND previously has reported on an increasing number of students leaving public schools because of the planned agenda, and O'Connell has warned districts they'll lose money if that happens.

A spokeswoman for a ministry called Considering Homeschooling said she already has seen an overwhelming increase in requests for information about homeschooling.

As a result, spokeswoman Denise Kanter told WND that her group is sending out 5,000 DVD packages to churches around the state that include basic "how-to" information to provide parents a direction to turn when they choose to protect their children from the new school agenda.

Another group's Web site, Discover Christian Schools, has been getting almost 4,000 visits per day as parents seek alternatives, co-founder Harold Naylor Jr. said.

The new law demands, "No teacher shall give instruction nor shall any school district sponsor any activity that promotes a discriminatory bias because of a characteristic [including perceived gender.]"

"With the passing of S.B.777, a Christian parent cannot, in good conscience, send their child to a public school where their child will be taught or coerced into a lifestyle or belief system that is contrary to the faith they hold dear," Kanter told WND.

In California, several parents told the Inland Valley *Press Enterprise* they were pulling their children from public school classrooms in protest of the law.

"We have rights, too. Enough is enough," Donna Myeres said.

Cause for Alarm

Randy Thomasson, president of the Campaign for Children and Families, said there is reason for alarm. He said the new law effectively requires school instruction and school activities to portray homosexuality, bisexuality and transsexuality to the six million children in public schools in a positive light.

He said he's gotten hundreds of contacts from concerned parents, and is encouraging families to leave the public school system entirely.

All of this has O'Connell alarmed.

In a notice to school superintendents, he said, "There may be fiscal consequences to school districts for funds lost due to student absences."

Meredith Turney, the legislative liaison for Capitol Resource Institute, reacted to that in a column.

"Mr. O'Connell, the bill's author Sen. Sheila Kuehl and Gov. Schwarzenegger have all maintained the party line that S.B.777 merely 'streamlines' existing anti-discrimination laws. However, these attempts to discredit the public outcry against S.B.777's policies are disingenuous and misleading. In fact, S.B.777 goes far beyond implementing anti-discrimination and harassment policies for public schools."

"The terms 'mom and dad' or 'husband and wife' could promote discrimination against homosexuals if a same-sex couple is not also featured," said Turney.

"Parents want the assurance that when their children go to school they will learn the fundamentals of reading, writing, and arithmetic—not social indoctrination regarding alternative sexual lifestyles. Now that S.B.777 is law, schools will in fact become indoctrination centers for sexual experimentation," she said.

As WND has reported, the non-profit Advocates for Faith and Freedom has filed a lawsuit challenging S.B.777.

Robert Tyler, the general counsel, said the lawsuit his organization has filed challenges the law on the basis it is unconstitutionally vague and violates the privacy of all students, teachers and other people on school campuses.

VIEWPOINT 3

> *"The exposure of the homosexual lifestyle to these children can . . . serve . . . as a reverberating moral value."*

Sex Education Programs Should Teach That Homosexuality Is Natural

Tenesha Curtis

In the following viewpoint, Tenesha Curtis argues that sexual education courses in middle school and high school should include information about homosexuality, including "safe sex" practices for both homosexual and heterosexual students. By middle school, she contends, students are beginning to recognize their own sexual orientations, and they need to understand the full range of human potential if they are to find their place in it. Schools must not indoctrinate but offer objective information, she concludes, so that parents can incorporate that information into their private moral teaching. Curtis is an essayist and poet who writes for the Web site Helium.

As you read, consider the following questions:

1. According to Gomez et al., why is high school not too early to talk about homosexuality?

Tenesha Curtis, "Should Education on Homosexuality Be Added to Sex Education in Schools?" www.helium.com., 2008. Reproduced by permission.

2. Why is learning about homosexuality beneficial to heterosexual students, according to the author?
3. How is teaching about homosexuality like teaching about evolution, according to the author?

Middle school is a time when sexuality and sexual choices become real social issues due to the onset of puberty and the introduction of sexual education into the curriculum. This is a point in the child's life when everything around them is being sorted and labeled, namely themselves and their peers. There's no legitimate reason to focus on heterosexuality alone when talking about safe sexual practices. In fact, doing so can be seen as quite harmful. [Jose] Gomez et al. make note of that in answer to a question about how even high school may be "too early" to have this discussion:

> "A majority of [heterosexual and homosexual] boys and girls are sexually active before they are 18 years old, and teenage boys are much more sexually active at this time than at any other period in their lives. Withholding information about sex is a form of sexual neglect, for which we pay great social costs such as unwanted teenage pregnancies, teenage VD [venereal disease], violence against gays, and so forth."

Gomez et al. also speak about a method of integration and ways of speaking that help the topic of homosexuality not stick out so much once being spoken of in the classroom:

> "It is extremely effective to integrate the topic of homosexuality throughout the family life/health education curriculum. Homosexuality may be introduced and considered when talking about sex roles, parenting, venereal diseases, prejudice, relationships, and legal issues. This may happen quite naturally, just by changing a word or two. For example, when talking about the relationships, refer to a couple as partners or lovers rather than as husband and wife or girlfriend and boyfriend. Thus, the discussion is no longer lim-

> ited to heterosexual behavior. When talking about venereal diseases, explain that gay people also get these diseases. When discussing, prejudices, stereotypes, or social relationships, remember to include attitudes towards homosexuality."

Including Homosexuality Offers Benefits

If a child is beginning to feel that they aren't attracted to members of the opposite sex, hearing only about the methods and safe sex of male-female copulation can lead to (sub)conscious feelings of ostracism, loneliness, and sadness as they realize that, besides not being able to relate to their same-sex peers sexually, they aren't even mentioned when it comes to sex, which is already supposed to be a risqué issue to discuss in school. But if homosexuals are included, there are three main, major benefits to be reaped. First, the bitter, depressing emotions a homosexual would experience at not being noted are eradicated. They don't get the impression that having feelings for persons of the same sex is completely unheard of or totally off the wall. Secondly, they understand that they too have a responsibility to have safe sex, no matter who they practice it with. This way, even though they are recognized as a sub-culture with its own practices, they are still classified as part of the broader, general population in the aspect of preventing the spread of disease. Thirdly, they are actually being educated on how to have safe-sex "their way." This can help cut down on sexual violence and the spreading of diseases since, because of the stigma attached to their sexual orientation, the child may try to find someone older than them that they don't know or with as little experience as them to experiment with. The point is that this person that the child has chosen could either not care about the younger person's safety, or not know any better how to go about having sex safely.

Beyond these gains to the homosexual adolescent, there are also up-sides for the heterosexuals of the class. First, they

Health Education Ignores Homosexual Students

Gay, lesbian, bisexual, and transgender (GLBT) students are more likely than their heterosexual peers to suffer health risks, including substance abuse, depression, and suicide, due to some extent to the continuing violence and harassment they experience. During the past decade, more students have publicly identified themselves as GLBT, serving to increase the pressure on schools to serve their needs, given that "all students deserve an opportunity for learning and healthy development in a safe and supportive environment." Yet, abstinence-only has become the primary emphasis of sexuality education, thus reducing any discussion of birth control, sexually transmitted diseases, sexual orientation, and other topics associated with comprehensive sex education.

Due to its controversial nature, the policy-making process surrounding sexuality education, and particularly programs involving sexual orientation, has become increasingly politicized. Heated debates over gay-straight student alliances, inclusion of GLBT youth in important school functions such as proms, and sexuality orientation education illustrate the extent to which public schools have become a battleground within the culture war conflicts of the United States. Single-issue groups have mobilized both for and against school policies related to these issues. Yet in many school curricula and policies, gays seemingly do not exist. This omission contributes to homophobia. Heterosexual students are given no reasons not to hate gays, while GLBT students are given no reasons not to hate themselves.

Barbara A. Rienzo, James W. Button, Jiunn-jye Sheu and Ying Li,
Journal of School Health, *March 2006, vol. 76, no. 3 p. 93.*

don't disregard the presence of homosexuals in their lives and become more conscious of the things that they do and say, that way they are less likely to offend a homosexual, or make them feel bad about their sexual preference which can help save a lot of relationships, as I spoke of earlier. Secondly, they are much less likely to be perpetrators of hate crimes and harassment or abuse in their school which of course can lead to reprimands, suspension, and expulsion. Thirdly, the seed of tolerance is subliminally implanted in them so that they can exercise the values of tolerance around their family and other peer groups, such as Scout troops and sports teams, therefore spreading the mindset and reinforcing their ability to get through life respecting people that are different from them in various ways.

The exposure of the homosexual lifestyle to these children can also serve its purpose as a reverberating moral value during their working and higher educational career. At this point in life the child will also side-step getting into any legal and social incidents involving hate crime and harassment or abuse stemming from the perceived "threat" of another's sexuality. Beyond this they will also teach their own children to be tolerant of others, as they have been. Their initial tolerance of a lifestyle like homosexuality will help lead them to be accepting of other human social differences such as race, nationality, socioeconomic status, age, gender, religion, and physical ability.

Critics Object

This is an issue that has, of course, brought many critics forward. One criticism produced by Ed Vitagliano is "If a parent views homosexuality as wrong, what is the child to do with a contradictory message coming from another respected authority figure—the child's teacher?" In answer to that, one must understand that the purpose of teaching about homosexuals and homosexual tolerance is not to necessarily persuade the child that homosexuality is "right," "wrong," "good," or "bad."

The purposes of talking about homosexuality in schools are supposed to be as follows: First, to fully explain the definition of "homosexuality" objectively. This means making sure that the children understand that homosexuality is not a disease or a choice, and that they understand that just because a person is attracted to people of their same sex, doesn't mean that they aren't human or that they deserve any lesser treatment than any other human being. Secondly, to prepare the children for an aspect of society that they will no doubt encounter even before they reach college and the working world. With these drives in mind, the parent that believes homosexuality is "wrong" or "a sin" is still able to confront the child about what beliefs they have about homosexuals. The point Vitagliano is really trying to make is that the teaching about homosexuality in schools will threaten the system of intellectual hierarchy in the home. In other words, parents want to MAKE their children believe what they already believe and having the "other side" of an issue presented to a child may weaken the parents' argument. I suppose that if a parent wants to dictate their children in such a manner, this could indeed be construed as a problem. On that note, I'd have to counter with the example that evolution is being taught in many schools even though many Christian (and other religiously affiliated) parents don't believe in it. The only way to "remedy" this "problem" is to allow the child to make their own decision about how to treat other human beings. The parents should present what they think to the child and then leave the child to their own ponderings on the subject.

Anita Bryant, an anti-gay activist, states in [Ralph] Smith and [Russel] Windes *Progay/Antigay* that, "public approval of admitted homosexual teachers could encourage more homosexuality by inducing pupils into looking upon it as an acceptable lifestyle." This notion is echoed in other areas of Vitagliano's essay. By making this statement, Bryant has shown her own ignorance and bigotry due to the fact that she, wrongfully might I add, believes that homosexuality is a choice. She seems to think that all kids want is the go-ahead, and they'll all suddenly, magically become attracted to people of the same sex. These are exactly the kinds of ideas that teaching more about homosexuality at early ages will eliminate.

VIEWPOINT 4

"It is wrong to use the lives of our children as political footballs."

Sex Education Programs Should Not Teach That Homosexuality Is Natural

Michelle Turner

In the following viewpoint, Michelle Turner calls for the removal of a sex education curriculum adopted for the Montgomery County, Maryland, public schools in 2007. The curriculum promotes acceptance of homosexuality without explaining the value of traditional marriage, she contends, and discusses "safe sex" without thoroughly explaining the risks of any sex outside marriage. She concludes that the curriculum makes value judgments that run counter to the values of many families. Turner is the spokesperson for Citizens for a Responsible Curriculum, a grassroots group of parents and citizens organized to reform the sex education curriculum in Montgomery County.

As you read, consider the following questions:

1. For which school district was the contested sex education material originally written, according to the author?

Michelle Turner, "Citizens Group Critical of New Sex Ed Curriculum, Press Release," *Citizens for a Responsible Curriculum (CRC)*, January 9, 2007. Reproduced by permission.

2. As reported by Michelle Turner, how is transgenderism classified by the American Psychiatric Association?
3. Why was Montgomery County's former sex curriculum rejected, according to the author?

The new sex ed curriculum passed by [Maryland's] Montgomery County's Board of Education wins a failing grade according to Citizens for a Responsible Curriculum [CRC], a grassroots citizens group concerned with a curriculum that is more about sexual politics than with medical facts. Michelle Turner, CRC's president, is especially critical of the curriculum's increased emphasis on moral approval of alternative lifestyles; the decreased or even absent treatment of abstinence as a choice; sex not placed within context of marriage; and lack of viewpoint neutrality.

"That all five lessons of the curriculum focus on and promote homosexuality and don't even touch on the value of having a traditional family should tell parents of the enormous influence of sexual advocacy groups placed by the Board on the Citizens Advisory Committee (CAC)," according to Turner. She also says that the curriculum is factually inaccurate and is packed with unsupported statements that endanger the health of students.

CRC's next steps in regard to challenging the curriculum are under discussion, she says.

She points out that the material for the curriculum is drawn from an excerpt from a book by Holt *Lifetime Health*, written for one of the most liberal school districts in the country, Los Angeles. It was authored by a gay activist and contains glaring omissions on the health risks of homosexual behavior.

A Physician Warns of Bias

Dr. Jacobs, an infectious disease specialist, was upset by the bias on the committee, "I have found that MCPS [Montgomery County Public Schools] and the CAC avoid saying anything that could reflect negatively on homosexuality, regardless of the health risks. Both the school and the committee have rejected a petition signed by 270 Montgomery County physicians asking that the Surgeon General's statement against condom use in anal intercourse be included." The Surgeon General warns that: "Condoms provide some protections, but anal intercourse is simply too dangerous to practice." The petition and statement were rejected.

"It is wrong to use the lives of our children as political footballs. Forty-five percent of the deaths from AIDS infections in the U.S. are due to men having sex with men even though they are about 2 percent of the population," she continues. "To not warn the children of these risks is irresponsible."

CRC also points to the introduction of transgenderism as normal, natural, unchangeable, and healthy. Turner says it fails to note that transgenderism is classified as a mental disorder by the American Psychiatric Association. She objects to the unwarranted positive spin in the curriculum such as: "While cross-dressers change their clothes, transsexuals sometimes change their body by means of hormone therapy or sexual reassignment surgery to match how they feel." In fact, major reputable medical facilities such as Johns Hopkins University Hospital and the Cleveland Clinic no longer perform reassignment surgery because they consider it unsuccessful in treating transgenderism.

In 2005 CRC and Parents and Friends of Ex-Gays sued the Board in a U.S. District Court over the previous proposed sex ed curriculum, claiming that the Board presented homosexuality from only one point of view. Religious concerns about it were ridiculed or discounted. Students who disagreed with the Board's interpretation were to be labeled homophobic, narrow-minded and bigoted. "This same viewpoint discrimination exists in the new curriculum. It demands a moral approval of

The New Battleground

The Montgomery County, Md., public school system developed sexual-education curriculum for eighth- and tenth-graders which claimed that Jesus "said absolutely nothing at all about homosexuality" and that being homosexual is similar to being left-handed. It also noted that some Baptist churches once defended racial segregation—implying that conservative Baptists today are wrong in opposing homosexuality. The pro-family legal group Liberty Counsel filed suit on behalf of two conservative groups and concerned parents, and in May a federal judge ruled against the school system, preventing the course from going into effect.

"Many of the leaders of the homosexual lobbying groups have admitted that they're targeting public schools," Mike Johnson, an attorney with the Alliance Defense Fund, told *Baptist Press*. "That is where they're trying to change society's perception of their activities and their behavior. That's the best place to do it—to go to the next generation. That's how you change minds and that's how you affect the culture. Sadly, they've had some success there."

Michael Foust, "Are Public Schools the Next Battleground over Heterosexuality?" Baptist Press, *June 7, 2005.*

some sexual conditions and practices that run counter to the teachings of many religions and certainly all the major ones," Turner voiced.

In addition, scientific and fact-based material on former homosexuals was specifically excluded. The judge in the case found this also was viewpoint discrimination, but before the case went to trial the Board threw out the curriculum and agreed to start from scratch. It formed a new committee, which then developed the present curriculum.

"In many ways this curriculum is more radical than the previous one. It certainly contains many of the elements we sued over in the first place," says Turner.

Value Judgments in the New Curriculum

CRC says it is important that parents know what the MCPS will begin teaching this spring [2007] in six schools, as part of the new curriculum pilot program. The curriculum includes these value judgments:

- "Homophobia is a fear or hatred of people believed to be homosexual. The term is used broadly to describe any range of negative attitudes toward or about gays, lesbians, bisexuals or transgender people. Homophobia may be shown in ways as mild as laughing at a gay joke or as severe and violent as gay bashing or murder,"
- "Like any other prejudice, homophobia is learned. Children are not born hating; they learn to hate and fear from messages they receive while growing up,"
- "For many people, coming out is liberating and empowering and makes them feel whole, healthy and complete,"
- "Most people who are gay, lesbian, or bi-sexual report feeling 'different' at a young age even though they may not have had a name for that feeling,"

Children will read and analyze four stories developed by a gay advocacy group:

1. Esperanza: "When I was a little girl . . . my grandfather would read me a bedtime story. . . . Sometimes he would read fairy tales about a beautiful princes and a charming prince . . . I knew that when I grew up, I would marry the beautiful princess, not the prince,"
2. Michael: "I was gay. . . . The pain of lying became so great that I started using drugs,"

3. Adrianne: "I've had great relationships with men and with woman. The hardest part about being bisexual is that people think I am confused. I can feel equally fulfilled and content with a man or with a woman,"
4. Portia: "I was supposed to be a boy, but every feeling inside told me that I was a girl . . . my parents and I had long talks . . . We had a meeting with the principal. I explained to her . . . that I wanted to be known as a girl and not use my birth name . . . the principal was incredible. . . . She gave me a new student ID and a key to the teachers' single stall restroom. Few transgender youths get the support that I was fortunate to receive,"

No heterosexual stories were included.

Viewpoint

> *"The Clubs, which are increasingly backed by teachers and administrators, provide a safe place for gay and gay-friendly students to socialize and support each other."*

Schools Should Permit Students to Form Gay-Straight Alliances

John Caldwell

In the following viewpoint, John Caldwell describes Gay-Straight Alliances (GSAs) and other high school clubs that attempt to create a supportive climate for homosexual students. These clubs are important, he argues, because they help homosexual students find peer groups without criticism and bullying, an experience many adult heterosexuals say they did not have in adolescence. As more schools support GSAs, he concludes, gay and straight students are becoming more comfortable with each other. Associate news editor of the Advocate, *a national gay and lesbian news magazine, Caldwell won the Sarah Pettit Memorial Award from the Lesbian and Gay Journalist Association in 2005.*

John Caldwell, "Gay Straight Revolution," The *Advocate*, June 21, 2005, pp. 69–70.

As you read, consider the following questions:

1. Why was the principal of Bear Creek High School in Colorado interested in forming a GSA, as reported in the viewpoint?
2. When was GLSEN formed, according to the author?
3. As described in the viewpoint, what happens during a Day of Silence protest?

When Javier Lopez arrived at Patrick Henry High School in Minneapolis as a freshman [in 2004] he had already told his parents he is gay and was ready to come out at school. But like many gay teens first grappling with the reality of being different, he was scared of what might happen. The urban school seemed a friendly enough place, but there was no obvious support system for gay students. So Lopez held off.

That was until a lesbian teacher, who said she understood what it was like to be a closeted teen, befriended Lopez, and together they formed a Gay-Straight Alliance—a school club in which gay students and their friends could come together. They set up a booth at the school's "information day" and got a few students to sign up. Now Lopez, who is 16 and a sophomore, is president of the group. And he is happy. "If there wasn't a GSA [a Gay-Straight Alliance], I probably wouldn't be out in high school," he says. "When I realized there was something there that could help, then I felt safe."

Jessica Jarrell, a 16-year-old junior at Bear Creek High School in suburban Lakewood, Colo., had a similar experience. Her principal was tired of hearing students utter antigay epithets in the halls and pushed the idea of forming a GSA. "She told the administration, 'This is what your students have to put up with,' and said they need to do something about it," says Jarrell. Soon the club was formed, and Jarrell was its enthusiastic leader.

A Quite Revolution

As a small number of students generate headlines with high-profile battles against parents and school officials over forming GSAs in some rural areas, there's a quiet revolution of gay clubs forming in high schools across the country. Over 3,000 GSAs now exist nationwide, with chapters in all fifty states, and while that accounts for only about 15 percent of the nation's high schools, the number is growing almost every day. Gay teens once wary of coming out now might encounter posters in high school hallways advertising the activities of other gay students. The clubs, which are increasingly backed by teachers and administrators, provide a safe place for gay and gay-friendly students to socialize and support each other.

And they are grooming the next generation of gay activists, who are ready to fight for full equality without hesitation. On-campus awareness campaigns, teacher training programs, and organized rallies for gay rights on and off school grounds are just a few of the activities a typical GSA might coordinate. "There's a new generation of LGBT [lesbian, gay, bisexual, transgendered] kids who are refusing to be treated like second-class citizens," says Kevin Jennings, 42, executive director for the Gay, Lesbian, and Straight Education Network [GLSEN], which facilitates the formation of the clubs. "Ten years ago the adults were ahead of the students. Now the students are ahead."

The blueprint for GSAs was established in the late 1980s, when Jennings was a teacher at a private high school in Boston. A gay student there told him he didn't think life was worth living. "I developed a philosophy that every gay student was my kid," Jennings says. "I did a talk at my school about being gay, and a girl came up to me and said she wanted to start a club to help gay kids. She said her mother was a lesbian and she was tired of hearing her family get put down at the school. She said, 'I'm straight and you're gay, so let's call it a gay-straight alliance.' That was 1988."

Gay-Straight Alliance Activities

From rural to urban settings, from east coast to west, GSAs around the country provide students with support and positive role models. The clubs channel teen energies from combating isolation to promoting education and increasing understanding.

"The Trinity (New York City) School GSA holds lunch meetings and sees films after school," teacher-adviser David Murphy told *Education World*. "We visit art galleries and attend national and local conferences. The students present workshops at those conferences and prepare school assembly programming."

"Spectrum [the North Olmsted, Ohio, GSA] meets three times per month at our off-campus location and once a month at school," said adviser Meara. "We have group discussions about confronting homophobia respectfully, and we host educational speakers. We lobbied the school board to amend the anti-harassment and anti-discrimination policies to include sexual orientation [with partial success]. We have organized observances of events such as National Coming Out Day, Day of Silence [a nationally organized show of solidarity with gay youth who can not speak out], and UN World AIDS Day."

Leslie Bulion,
"Gay-Straight Alliances: Ground Zero for School Tolerance,"
June 29, 2007. www.educationworld.com.

Jennings formed GLSEN in 1990 and four years later left his teaching job to become the group's first executive director, helping GSAs form nationwide. "The great thing about GSAs is how remarkable they are, and how unremarkable," says Jennings, who now lives in New York City with his partner of ten years, Jeffrey Davis. "Students are sitting around talking and having pizza. So many gay people in our generation didn't get to have their adolescence until their 20s. These young people are getting to have it now."

Opportunities for Activism

That's true for Lopez, who says his club is a diverse group of friends who get a lot done but also have fun just hanging out. After they put together a National Coming Out Day event earlier this year, in which club members handed out stickers and "chalked" the school sidewalk with pro-gay messages, they held a party, he says. The club has participated in several of GLSEN's "Days of Action," including the Day of Silence protest and the Transgender Day of Remembrance, and they went to the state capitol for a rally against Minnesota's proposed ban on same-sex marriage. "But we're also doing some fun events like movie night and going to a coffee shop," he says.

That kind of safe and fun environment is also available to Cory Ashby, 17, even if not through an official GSA. Administrators and parents at Winterset High School in his rural Iowa town of about 5,000 aren't receptive to the idea of an official gay club. But as in the case of Lopez, one of Ashby's teachers—who has a gay brother—stepped in to help, and now they have a "diversity club." "This year we participated in all of GLSEN's Days of Action," he says. "It's not really an official club, but we're very active. It's a group of like-minded people who want to come together for common goals. The majority of the people who come to the meetings are straight. They are so willing to reach out and help, even though it's kind of scary in this place."

Ashby, Jarrell, and Lopez all have been to GLSEN's leadership training, a summer conference held last year in Washington, D.C., where they learned how to coordinate activities, organize workshops, and raise awareness among school officials. And whether they are able to form a GSA or not, what they bring back to their schools is making a difference. Amid some controversy around the Day of Silence protest Ashby recently organized, in which gay students and their allies remain silent for the day in order to raise awareness about the silence gays have had to endure, Ashby's principal called him into his office. "He was supportive," says Ashby, who plans on joining the Peace Corps after attending Knox College in Illinois beginning next year. "It's really raised awareness. There's resistance, but the people who want to do it are willing to go against the current."

Most of the resistance to Jarrell's club comes from outside the school. One of her friends was kicked out of his house after his parents found out he was going to the GSA, and another was pulled out of school because his parents decided there were too many gay people there.

But in school, resistance is fading, she says. "The first year of our GSA, one of the student's cars got spray-painted with the word 'fag,'" says Jarrell, who will graduate early and study art history at the University of Colorado at Denver this fall. "That same year a student was harassed in a parking lot. But now things like that don't happen as often. Our GSA has drastically improved our school."

And as for the once timid Lopez, who debated the risks of coming out: "Now everyone knows my name at school," he says "If there's ever a GSA question, they say, 'Go talk to Javier.'"

"Is it worth pointing out, even at this late date, that the teachers and administrators were right about the dangers of labeling—and wrong when they allowed and encouraged homosexual students to be labeled?"

Schools Should Not Permit Students to Form Gay-Straight Alliances

Paul Scalia

In the following viewpoint, Paul Scalia explains that groups such as Gay-Straight Alliances promote labeling and encourage students to fix their sexuality when in fact they may just be confused. Scalia says that high school is a time students are figuring out their bodies and sexuality is in flux. When students are forced to identify with a group, they may be stuck with a label that is ultimately harmful. Paul Scalia is a priest of the Diocese of Arlington, Virginia, and chaplain for the Arlington chapter of Courage.

Paul Scalia, "A Label That Sticks (Opinion)," *First Things: A Monthly Journal of Religion and Public Life*, June-July 2005. Reproduced by permission.

As you read, consider the following questions:

1. According to the viewpoint, what was President Bush's response when asked if homosexuality was inherited or chosen?
2. Does the author believe that people's sexual inclinations determine their identity?
3. What are two of the arguments Scalia presents against labeling?

When I was in high school, the students fell into many different groups: preps, jocks, cheerleaders, punks, deadheads, druggies, geeks, and all the rest. Just about everyone received an unofficial but virtually unchangeable assignment to a particular group. When I work in high schools today, I discover little difference. The groups still exist (with just a few changes in terminology), and the teachers and administrators still counsel against the labels. As they wisely explain, labels reinforce stereotypes and prejudices; they prevent us from accepting individuals and getting to know the real person.

The Dangers of Labeling

There is one difference, however. While still warning children against stereotypes and labels, high-school administrations increasingly encourage one group of students to label themselves: those who experience same-sex attractions. With the assistance (and sometimes pressure) of such groups as the Gay-Straight Alliance [GSA] and the Gay, Lesbian, and Straight Education Network [GLSEN] high schools across the country now routinely have student organizations dedicated to promoting the tolerance and acceptance of homosexuality. Indeed, New York City has an entire school—Harvey Milk High School—devoted to "gay, lesbian, transgendered and questioning youth."

Is it worth pointing out, even at this late date, that the teachers and administrators were right about the dangers of labeling—and wrong when they allowed and encouraged homosexual students to be labeled? As with most errors, this one proceeds from a certain truth and often from good intentions. The truth is that adolescents with same-sex attractions have a higher suicide rate and are more likely to abuse alcohol and drugs. Attributing these problems to persecution and harassment, the new groups pledge to create a safe atmosphere so that students will not be tempted to self-destructive behavior.

But in practice this agenda means more than just an end to the name-calling. It means the approval of homosexuality and, in a new form of name-calling, an insistence that adolescents who experience same-sex attractions "come out" as homosexual.

This is, to begin with, a failure of common sense. Such categorizations feed into the adolescent penchant for labels. High-school students want to belong to a group. They want an identity. Getting to know other people, figuring them out, sorting out who you are in light of who they are—that can be difficult work. Labels make it much easier. Many adolescents latch on to an identity for a time and then think better of it later. For this reason parents and teachers traditionally guard against pigeonholing students in certain categories.

The new approach, however, does just the opposite. It encourages labeling. Rather than struggle through the difficulties of adolescence, a high-school freshman or sophomore can now, with official support, profess to be gay—and he instantly has an identity and a group. Now he belongs. He knows who he is. Gone is the possibility that adolescents might be confused, perhaps even wrong. Adults typically display a wise reserve about the self-discoveries of high-school students: they know adolescents are still figuring things out, and they recognize their responsibility to help sort through the confusion. So why is all this natural wisdom somehow abandoned these days—in the most confused and confusing area of adolescent sexuality?

Of course, the phrases are tempting because of their convenience and efficiency. They are common, close at hand, and make quick work of a difficult issue. But they also identify an individual person with his homosexual inclinations. They presume that a person is his inclinations or attractions; he is a "gay" or is a "homosexual." At some point adults have to admit that a fifteen-year-old who claims to be "a questioning transgendered bisexual" is really just confused.

Consequences of Confusion

Meanwhile, the schools' endorsement of all this quickly undermines parents' authority in an extraordinarily sensitive area. While the parents try to teach one thing at home, the school presents the opposite view, now not only in the classroom but also socially (which in high school might have a greater effect). And those parents who have a better way to handle their child's difficulties will find their efforts thwarted. At home, they strive to love their children, help them in their struggles, and teach a coherent truth about human sexuality. Meanwhile at school, children receive the propaganda and encouragement to argue precisely against what their parents say.

Much of this social engineering rests on the view that homosexuality is a fixed, inborn orientation. The school groups hold this as a dogma not open for discussion. In one of the presidential debates last year, when asked if he thought homosexuality was inherited or chosen, President Bush wisely and modestly answered that he did not know. With that he showed himself to be fairly well aligned with the scientific community, which itself cannot produce a uniform answer to the question. The supposed "gay gene" has never been proven or discovered. The most we can say is that certain people may have genetic predispositions towards homosexuality—which is a far cry from saying they inherit it.

The high-school organizations, however, have no qualms about pronouncing the matter settled. Insisting that homo-

GSAs Do Not Provide "Safe Schools"

Teenagers' same-sex attractions do not automatically mean that they are homosexual. Many teens go through temporary episodes of idealization of same-sex peers and should not be urged to prematurely label themselves as "gay." Most parents hope to maximize the likelihood of their child growing up to be heterosexual and comfortable in claiming his or her own masculine or feminine nature. Teens themselves have the right to be presented with all information. But instead of presenting all of the facts on sexual orientation in a fair and balanced manner, GLSEN (Gay, Lesbian, and Straight Education Network), GSAs (Gay-Straight Alliances), PFLAG (Parents, Families and Friends of Lesbians & Gays), and other anti-ex-gay groups encourage confused and impressionable youth to immediately identify as "gay" and thus, ensure a future homosexual outcome that may be unnecessary. Indeed, they would deny a student's right to receive information on alternatives for unwanted same-sex attractions. Is this what our children deserve?

"How to Respond to a Gay/Straight Alliance (GSA) Club,"
Parents and Friends of Ex-Gays and Gays,
Nov. 14, 2006. http://pfox.org.

sexuality is inborn, they immediately conclude that an adolescent with homosexual inclinations must necessarily be homosexual, or gay, or lesbian, or transgendered—whichever label fits.

And once the label is assigned, it is awfully hard to remove. It lasts past high school and leaves the adolescent at the mercy of our culture's extremes. What man of you, if his son asks him for bread, will give him a stone? Or if he asks for a fish, will give him a serpent? Increasingly, our high schools distribute stones and serpents to hungry children. Adolescents legitimately confused or anxious about their sexuality receive the advice to assume the homosexual label, truncating their identities perhaps for their entire lives.

Given the obvious errors of this new approach, the question still remains, especially for parents: How should one respond to adolescents with same-sex attractions? Love must be the leading edge of the response. The school organizations attract adolescents precisely because they pledge unconditional acceptance and affirmation of the person, no matter what "orientation" he has. Never mind that receiving this acceptance and affirmation in effect requires signing up for the gay agenda, adolescents still perceive it as acceptance and affirmation. Parents need to understand how effective this is. The first point to make known, then, is not what is wrong but what is right: The child is lovable, and is loved. That love, more than anything else, instills in adolescents the trust and confidence they need to struggle with whatever painful and saddening realities they face.

Love the Child, Reject the Actions

Difficulties arise when the child insists on being accepted and loved not as a person but as a "gay," "homosexual," or "other"—when he wants to be loved according to the label. And our culture willingly indulges these labels for the same reason we used them in high school: We find it easier to deal with labels than with actual persons. Clearly this situation demands tremendous patience and perseverance; it requires parents to insist continually that, no, their child is not just the sum of his sexual attractions, that they can love their child while rejecting some of his actions.

Adolescents need to hear precisely this: People's sexual inclinations do not determine their identity. Nor does every so-called "homosexual" feel attractions of the same character or to the same degree. Some have strong and lasting homosexual desires; for others, such desires are slight and passing. Lumping everyone together as having the same orientation or identity is a grotesque reduction of a complicated reality, and it massively damages the very people it claims to help.

Resisting the labeling temptation demands that we reject the culture's vocabulary and adopt more precise terms. In popular usage, the words "gay" and "lesbian" imply a fixed orientation and the living out of a lifestyle. Even the term "homosexual person," which is used in some Vatican documents, suggests that homosexual inclinations somehow determine, which is to say confine, a person's identity.

Granted, the more accurate phrases do not trip easily off the tongue. But what is lost in efficiency is gained in precision. Terms such as "same-sex attractions" and "homosexual inclinations" express what a person experiences without identifying the person with those attractions. They both acknowledge the attractions and preserve the freedom and dignity of the person. With that essential distinction made, parents can better oppose the attractions without rejecting the child. And as the child matures, he will not find his identity confined to his sexuality.

Understanding the Full Truth of Human Sexuality

Further, opposition to homosexual attractions and actions makes sense only when it is rooted in the full truth of human sexuality. Gay school groups gain approval and support partly because heterosexual unchastity (contraception, masturbation, premarital sex, adultery, and all the rest) has compromised so many. Our culture's deliberate separation of sex from procreation has destroyed our ability to articulate a coherent explanation of sexual ethics. Parents and educators have damaged the tools that would allow them to explain why homosexual activity is wrong.

Understanding the full truth of human sexuality produces an appreciation for purity. Of course, all young people need to strive for this virtue. But purity takes on a greater significance for those with same-sex attractions. Nothing will confirm a supposed "gay" identity more quickly and solidly than homosexual actions. After a homosexual encounter, the adolescent must either admit the error of his actions and repent—or more boldly identify himself with his actions and look for a way to justify them.

As sexual license increases in our culture, we will encounter more adolescents confused about their sexuality and perhaps experiencing same-sex attractions. The easy option is to dissolve the tension by approving homosexuality and even encouraging it. But the most charitable thing we can do for such youth is to love them as God's own images, to teach them the full truth about human sexuality, and to enable them to live it. Anything less is giving our children stones when they ask for bread.

Periodical Bibliography

The following articles have been selected to supplement the diverse views presented in this chapter.

Heather Barber and Vikki Krane	"Creating a Positive Climate for Lesbian, Gay, Bisexual, and Transgender Youths," *Journal of Physical Education, Recreation and Dance*, September 2007.
Time	"The Battle over Gay Teens,", October 10, 2005.
Marilyn Elias	"Gay Teens Coming Out Earlier to Peers and Family," *USA Today*, February 8, 2007.
Tom Mountain	"Nightmare at Franklin," *Newton Tab*, November 8, 2006.
Mark Harris	"A Lovely Outing: J.K. Rowling's Revelation of Professor Albus Dumbledore," *Entertainment Weekly*, November 2, 2007.
Linda Harvey	"Christian Parents: Stop Trusting Harry Potter," October 24, 2007. www.worldnetdaily.com.
Jill M. Hermann-Wilmarth	"Full Inclusion," *Language Arts*, March 2007.
Carrie Kilman	"This Is Why We Need a GSA," *Teaching Tolerance*, Spring 2007.
Loren Krywanczyk	"Queering Public School Pedagogy as a First-Year Teacher," *Radical Teacher*, Summer 2007.
Ian K. Macgillivray	"Religion, Sexual Orientation, and School Policy," *Educational Studies*, January 2008.
Elizabeth H. Rowell	"Missing!: Picture Books Reflecting Gay and Lesbian Families," *Young Children*, May 2007.
Diana Jean Shemo	"Lessons on Homosexuality Move into the Classroom," *New York Times*, August 15, 2007.

For Further Discussion

Chapter 1

1. Robert Mitchum and Neil Swidey begin their viewpoints with anecdotes about individuals, and use a conversational writing style in their viewpoints. On the other hand, the Richard Fitzgibbons viewpoint does not include narratives, and relies on more general examples and psychological terms to make its points. In making an argument about an issue like homosexuality, which for many people is both a rational and an emotional topic, what are the benefits and drawbacks of each approach to writing?
2. List all of the possible causes for homosexuality suggested by the viewpoints in this chapter. In your opinion, which ones seem the most likely? Which seem the least likely? Why?
3. In his viewpoint, Andrew Fink argues that it does not matter what causes homosexuality. Why, in your opinion, are many people so eager to identify an indisputable cause? What results would follow from an agreement that sexual orientation is a choice, or that it is not a choice? Explain your answer.
4. In his viewpoint, the author writing as "Ben Newman" draws primarily on his own experiences to argue that homosexuality can be cured. In the opposing viewpoint, Casey Sanchez operates as a reporter, presenting information and opinions gathered through research and interviews. Does the source of information each draws on affect how you evaluate the viewpoints? Why or why not?

Chapter 2

1. Several of the viewpoints in this chapter discuss "unit cohesion," and the idea that service members should not have to serve—and cannot do their best work—in close contact with people who make them uncomfortable. Do you accept this premise? In a time of war, how should the government and the military weigh the wishes of gay men and women who want to serve their country with the conflicting wishes of men and women who prefer to serve without them?
2. Mackubin Thomas Owens, Robert Maginnis, and John McCain are all combat veterans. The other authors in this chapter, Gregory M. Herek, Aaron Belkin, C. Dixon Osburn, and Laura Kiritsy, are not veterans but scholars and reporters who have studied the issues from the outside. Does an author's own combat experience or lack of experience affect how you read the viewpoints? Explain your answer.
3. In her viewpoint, Laura Kiritsy tells stories of gay men and women who have served in the armed forces, and argues that sexual orientation does not affect a person's bravery or dedication. Mackubin Thomas Owens and John McCain argue that the presence of gay men and women in a combat unit weakens that unit. Can both perspectives be right? Use evidence from the viewpoints to explain your answer.

Chapter 3

1. In her viewpoint, Congresswoman Marilyn Musgrave brings up opposing arguments, and then explains why those arguments are unconvincing. Do you find this strategy effective? Why or why not?
2. In their viewpoints, Charles Krauthammer and Dennis O'Brien focus on abstractions—the role of federal versus state government, or the philosophical underpinnings of

our legal and moral codes—rather than on practical, day-to-day effects of marriage and family. How do these abstract ideas help shape your understanding of the more practical questions? Or do they? Explain your answer.

3. Midge Decter uses strong language in her viewpoint, writing of "assault," "lying," "misguided enablers," "a culture grown sick," and "a spit in the eye." Does this type of language affect the way you respond to her arguments? If so, how?
4. The man writing as "An Adoptive Father" and the co-authors William Meezan and Jonathan Rauch agree that the needs of children must come first when thinking about adoption. What else do they agree on?
5. In Chapter 1, Andrew Fink argues that the causes of homosexuality are irrelevant—that it is more important to deal with the reality of what people are than worry about how they got that way. In this chapter, Mary E. Hunt argues that the institution of marriage is in some ways irrelevant—that it is more important to support the ways people actually live and form families than to try to categorize those family relationships. What effects do these authors expect their arguments will have on their readers? If they do not anticipate changing the direction of large societal debates, what is their purpose?

Chapter 4

1. In his viewpoint, Arthur Lipkin argues, among other things, that teenagers want to learn about sexuality in school. Bob Unruh argues, on the other hand, that parents are better judges than their children of which educational topics are appropriate. How much involvement should teenagers have making decisions about their education? What factors should be considered in answering this question?

2. Some of the viewpoints in this chapter describe a "homosexual lobby" that is actively trying to harm young people. These viewpoints, including those by Bob Unruh and Michelle Turner, use dramatic language that creates or draws upon parental fears. How does this approach affect the way you respond to the arguments in these viewpoints? Explain your answer.
3. In their viewpoints, Tanesha Curtis and Michelle Turner agree that including material about homosexuality in sex education classes is an attempt to teach a moral value. How do the two authors see this purpose differently? Use material from the viewpoint to explain your answer.
4. John Caldwell argues that forming gay-straight alliances is simply a way to make sure that gay and lesbian students are treated like other students, while Paul Scalia argues that these groups encourage students to give themselves permanent labels while their identities are still unformed. Whose argument is more convincing? Use examples from the viewpoints to develop your answer.

Organizations to Contact

The editors have compiled the following list of organizations concerned with the issues debated in this book. The descriptions are derived from materials provided by the organizations. All have publications or information available for interested readers. The list was compiled on the date of publication of the present volume; the information provided here may change. Be aware that many organizations take several weeks or longer to respond to inquiries, so allow as much time as possible.

American Family Association (AFA)
PO Drawer 2440, Tupelo, MS 38803
(662)844-5036
Web site: www.afa.net

A nonprofit organization founded in 1917, the American Family Association (AFA) stands for traditional family values, focusing primarily on the influence of television and other media. Although it works to expose the misrepresentation of the radical homosexual agenda and stop its spread, AFA also sponsors events reaching out to homosexuals and promoting Christian love and healing. The monthly *AFA Journal* contains news on various moral and family issues. The Web site offers news, free online newsletters, posters and brochures for downloading, and action alerts.

Center for Military Readiness (CMR)
PO Box 51600, Livonia, MI 48151
(202)347-5333
e-mail: info@cmrlink.org
Web site: www.cmrlink.org

The Center for Military Readiness (CMR) is an independent, nonpartisan educational organization formed to take a leadership role in promoting sound military personnel policies in the armed forces. Among its issues, CMR advocates strict enforcement of the law banning open homosexuality in the military. The organization publishes a magazine, *CMR Notes*, ten times each year, as well as periodic reports. The Web site collects news articles and opinion pieces about homosexuals in the military dating back to 2001.

Citizens for Community Values (CCV)
11175 Reading Road, Suite 103, Cincinnati, OH 45241
(513)733-5775 • fax: (513)733-5794
Web site: www.ccv.org

Citizens for Community Values (CCV), which began as a grassroots organization to combat pornography in Cincinnati, Ohio, exists to promote Judeo-Christian moral values, and to reduce destructive behaviors contrary to those values, through education, active community partnership, and individual empowerment at the local, state and national levels. It coordinates the National Pro-Family Forum on Homosexuality, a group of national pro-family leaders who meet four times a year to defend traditional "one man-one woman" marriage. CCV publishes *Citizens' Courier*, an educational quarterly newsletter, while its Web site publishes periodic opinion columns and news articles, press releases, and a link to register for e-mail news, media statements, and alerts.

Exodus International
PO Box 540119, Orlando, FL 32854
(407)599-6872 or 888-264-0877
Web site: http://exodus.to

Exodus is a nonprofit, interdenominational Christian organization promoting the message of freedom from homosexuality through the power of Jesus Christ, and the largest Christian referral and information network dealing with homosexual issues in the world. The group publishes two monthly newsletters, *Exodus Update* and *The Exodus Impact*. Its Web site offers an online searchable library of articles on aspects of homosexuality from scientific and theological perspectives, first-person accounts from people who have struggled with homosexuality, and downloadable brochures and graphics.

Family Research Institute
PO Box 62640, Colorado Springs, CO 80962-2640
(303)681-3113
Web site: www.familyresearchinst.org

Family Research Institute, a nonprofit scientific and educational corporation, believes the strength of our society depends on preserving America's historic moral framework and the traditional family. FRI works to produce sound scientific data on pressing social issues—especially homosexuality—in an effort to promote traditional policies. The group publishes a monthly newsletter, *Family Research Report*, back issues of which are available online. The Web site also provides special reports, published articles, and pamphlets on the causes and the effects of homosexuality.

Focus on the Family
8605 Explorer Drive, Colorado Springs, CO 80920
(800)232-6459
Web site: www.focusonthefamily.com

Founded in 1977 by James Dobson, Focus on the Family is one of the largest evangelical groups in the United States. Its extensive outreach program includes a daily radio broadcast, and a variety of magazines, books, videos, and audio recordings. The Web site offers opinion columns, news articles, reports, and links to Focus on the Family-sponsored Web sites addressing specific topics, including troubledwith.com, addressing homosexuality under the heading "Love and Sex," and lovewonout.com, which sponsors conferences, education, counseling and research on escaping homosexuality.

Gay, Lesbian, and Straight Education Network (GLSEN)
90 Broad Street, 2nd Floor, New York, NY 10004
(212)727-0135
Web site: www.glsen.org

The Gay, Lesbian, and Straight Education Network (GLSEN) strives to assure that each member of every school community is valued and respected regardless of sexual orientation or gender identity/expression. The group sponsors gay-straight alliance clubs in schools, as well as events including "No Name-Calling Week" and the "Day of Silence," and conducts an annual survey on the climate for gay and lesbian students in their schools. On its Web site, GLSEN maintains a library of surveys, stories, news articles, lesson plans, and organizing materials

Human Rights Campaign
1640 Rhode Island Avenue, NW
Washington, DC 20036-3278
(800)777-4723 • fax: (202)347-5323

The Human Rights Campaign is America's largest civil rights organization working to achieve gay, lesbian, bisexual, and transgender [GLBT] equality. HRC works to secure equal rights for GLBT individuals and families at the federal and state levels by lobbying elected officials, mobilizing grassroots supporters, educating Americans, and investing strategically to elect fair-minded officials. The group publishes a quarterly magazine, *Equality*, and presents a weekly radio show and daily Web cast. Its Web site offers reports, an interactive map with state-specific news, and information about issues including coming out, the military, and parenting.

MassResistance
PO Box 1612, Waltham, MA 02454
(781)890-6001
Web site: www.massresistance.org

MassResistance, organized in 1995 as Parents' Rights Coalition, is the leading pro-family grassroots activist group in Massachusetts, although many of its issues and activities have national implications. MassResistance focuses its efforts on stopping legislation permitting same-sex marriage and education about homosexuality in schools. The organization presents programming on Radio Free Massachusetts, as well as special reports, news and feature stories and a blog, all available through the Web site.

National Association for Research & Therapy of Homosexuality (NARTH)
(888)364-4744
e-mail: nationalarth@yahoo.com
Web site: www.narth.com

The National Association for Research & Therapy of Homosexuality (NARTH) is a nonprofit, educational organization dedicated to affirming a complementary, male-female model of gender and sexuality. Founded in 1992, the group includes psychiatrists, psychologists, certified social workers, professional and pastoral counselors and other behavioral scientists, as well as laymen from a wide variety of backgrounds such as law, religion, and education. The organization publishes the *NARTH Bulletin* three times each year, and archives back issues on its Web site. Also available online are reports, commentaries, interviews, testimonials, and a recommended reading list, as well as a link for registering for e-mail updates.

Michael D. Palm Center
Aaron Belkin, Director, Santa Barbara, CA 93106-9420
(805)893-5664
Web site: www.palmcenter.org

The Michael D. Palm Center is a research institute at the University of California, Santa Barbara, which sponsors state-of-the-art research about critical and controversial issues of the day. The Center's priority, the "Don't Ask, Don't Tell" Project, continues the work of the former Center for the Study of Sexual Minorities in the Military. The Center publishes an online monthly newsletter, available through e-mail subscription, as well as reports, press releases, and links to other resources.

Parents, Families, and Friends of Lesbians and Gays (PFLAG)
PFLAG National Office, Washington, DC 20036
(202)467-8180 • fax: (202)467-8194
e-mail: info@pflag.org
Web site: http://community.pflag.org

Parents, Families, and Friends of Lesbians and Gays (PFLAG), a national organization with over 200,000 members and supporters and over five hundred affiliates in the United States, promotes the health and well-being of gay, lesbian, bisexual, and transgender persons, their families, and friends through support, education, and advocacy. The group maintains an online newsroom, and also provides tools for creating safe schools, as well as a variety of reports on issues including hate crimes, workplace discrimination, and the "Don't Ask, Don't Tell" policy.

Religious Tolerance

Ontario Consultants on Religious Tolerance
Watertown, NY 13601-0128 •fax: 613-547-9015
Web site: www.religioustolerance.org

Religious Tolerance is a multi-faith group whose mission is to explain the full diversity of religious beliefs in North America, including Buddhism, Christianity, Confucianism, Hinduism, Islam, Judaism, Taoism, Wicca, other spiritual groups. The organization's Web site attempts to describe all viewpoints on controversial religious topics objectively and fairly; issues include whether homosexuals and bisexuals should be given equal rights, including same-sex marriage. The site also offers an unmoderated online forum, lists of recommended books, and links to other religious sites.

Safe Schools Coalition

c/o Lifelong AIDS Alliance, Seattle, WA 98122-4203
(206)632-0662 • fax: (206)325-2689
Web site: www.safeschoolscoalition.org

The Safe Schools Coalition is an international public-private partnership in support of gay, lesbian, bisexual, and transgender youth. Its missions is to help schools become safe places where every family can belong, where every educator can teach, and where every child can learn, regardless of gender identity or sexual orientation. On its Web site the organization offers reports, posters, and handouts for teachers, for students, and for parents and guardians, as well as information about state, national, and international laws and policies.

Servicemembers Legal Defense Network (SLDN)
PO Box 65301, Washington, DC 20035-5301
(202)328-3244 or 202-328-FAIR • fax: (202)797-1635
e-mail: sldn@sldn.org
Web site: www.sldn.org

Servicemembers Legal Defense Network (SLDN) is a national, nonprofit legal services, watchdog and policy organization dedicated to ending discrimination against and harassment of military personnel affected by "Don't Ask, Don't Tell" and related forms of intolerance. It provides free legal services to service members harmed by "Don't Ask, Don't Tell" and related, discriminatory policies, and advocates for policies and practices that improve the lives of service members. The group's Web site collects press releases and news stories, and also publishes a blog and online forum, *The Frontline.*

Southern Poverty Law Center (SPLC)
400 Washington Avenue, Montgomery, AL 36104
(334)956-8200
Web site: www.splcenter.org

The Southern Poverty Law Center (SPLC) was founded in 1971 as a small civil rights law firm. Today, SPLC is internationally known for its tolerance education programs, its legal victories against white supremacists and its tracking of hate groups. The organization publishes an e-mail newsletter, as well as two print magazines: *Teaching Tolerance*, supporting the efforts of K-12 teachers and other educators to promote respect for differences and an appreciation of diversity; and the *Intelligence Report*, reporting on SPLC's progress in combating hate groups. The Web site also offers press releases, classroom tools, and a blog, *Hatewatch.*

Bibliography of Books

Robert Aldrich	*Gay Life and Culture: A World History*. New York: Universe, 2006.
Donald Altschiller	*Hate Crimes: A Reference Handbook*. Santa Barbara, CA: ABC-CLIO, 2005.
Eric Anderson	*In the Game: Gay Athletes and the Cult of Masculinity*. Albany, NY: State University of New York Press, 2005.
Mary Virginia Lee Badgett and Jeff Frank	*Sexual Orientation Discrimination: An International Perspective*. New York: Routledge, 2007.
Harry M. Benshoff and Sean Griffin	*Queer Images: A History of Gay and Lesbian Film in America*. Lanham, MD: Rowman & Littlefield, 2006.
David Blankenhorn	*The Future of Marriage*. New York: Encounter Books, 2007.
Kate Burns	*At Issue: Gay and Lesbian Families*. San Diego: Greenhaven Press, 2005.
Sean Cahill	*Same-Sex Marriage in the United States: Focus on the Facts*. Lanham, MD: Lexington Books, 2004.
Michael Cart and Christine Jenkins	*The Heart Has Its Reasons: Young Adult Literature with Gay/Lesbian/Queer Content, 1969–2004*. Lanham, MD: Scarecrow Press, 2006.
David Carter	*Stonewall: The Riots That Sparked the Gay Revolution*. New York: St. Martin's, 2004.

Jimmy Carter — *Our Endangered Values: America's Moral Crisis*. New York: Simon & Schuster, 2005.

George Chauncey — *Why Marriage? The History Shaping Today's Debate over Gay Equality*. Cambridge, MA: Basic Books, 2004.

Donald H. Clark — *Loving Someone Gay*. Berkeley, CA: Celestial Arts, 2005.

Carol Curoe and Robert Curoe — *Are There Closets in Heaven?: A Catholic Father and Lesbian Daughter Share Their Story*. Minneapolis, MN: Syren, 2007.

Joe Dallas — *When Homosexuality Hits Home: What to Do When a Loved One Says They're Gay*. Eugene, OR: Harvest House, 2004.

Joe Dallas — *The Gay Gospel? How Pro-Gay Advocates Misread the Bible*. Eugene, OR: Harvest House, 2007.

Melissa M. Deckman — *School Board Battles: The Christian Right in Local Politics*. Washington, DC: Georgetown University Press, 2004.

James Dobson — *Marriage under Fire: Why We Must Win this Battle*. Sisters, OR: Multnomah, 2004.

Alan Downs — *The Velvet Rage: Overcoming the Pain of Growing Up Gay in a Straight Man's World*. Cambridge, MA: Da Capo, 2006.

Robert L. Fatiggi — *What the Church Teaches about Sex: God's Plan for Happiness*. Huntington, IN: Our Sunday Visitor, 2008.

Ronnie W. Floyd — *The Gay Agenda: It's Dividing the Family, the Church, and a Nation*. Green Forest, AR: New Leaf Press, 2004.

Nancy Garden — *Hear Us Out!: Lesbian and Gay Stories of Struggle, Progress and Hope, 1950 to the Present*. New York: Farrar, Straus and Giroux, 2007.

Abigail Garner — *Families Like Mine: Children of Gay Parents Tell It Like It Is*. New York: HarperCollins, 2004.

Evan Gerstmann — *Same-Sex Marriage and the Constitution*. New York: Cambridge University Press, 2004.

Mark D. Jordan — *Blessing Same-Sex Unions: The Perils of Queer Romance and the Confusions of Christian Marriage*. Chicago, IL: University of Chicago Press, 2005.

Lisa Keen — *Out Law: What GLBT Youth Should Know about Their Legal Rights*. Boston, MA: Beacon, 2007.

Michael A. King — *Stumbling Toward a Genuine Conversation on Homosexuality*. Telford, PA: Cascadia, 2007.

Sylvain Larocque — *Gay Marriage: The Story of a Canadian Social Revolution*. Toronto, Ontario, Canada: James Lorimer, 2006.

Arthur Lipkin	*Beyond Diversity Day: A Q&A on Gay and Lesbian Issues in Schools.* Lanham, MD: Rowman and Littlefield, 2004.
Erwin W. Lutzer	*The Truth about Same-Sex Marriage: Six Things You Need to Know about What's Really at Stake.* Chicago, IL: Moody, 2004.
Francis MacNutt	*Can Homosexuality Be Healed?* Ada, MI: Chosen, 2006.
Meredith Maran and Angela Watrous	*50 Ways to Support Lesbian and Gay Equality: The Complete Guide to Supporting Family, Friends, Neighbors—or Yourself.* Maui, HI: Inner Ocean, 2005.
Eric Marcus	*Is It a Choice?* San Francisco, CA: HarperSanFrancisco, 2005
Eric Marcus	*What if Someone I Know Is Gay?* New York: Simon Pulse, 2007.
Jeffrey McGowan	*Major Conflict: One Gay Man's Life in the Don't-Ask-Don't-Tell Military.* New York: Broadway, 2005.
Dina Matos McGreevey	*Silent Partner: A Memoir of My Marriage.* New York: Hyperion, 2007.
Michael Mello	*Legalizing Gay Marriage.* Philadelphia, PA: Temple University Press, 2004.
Nell Miller	*Out of the Past: Gay and Lesbian History from 1869 to the Present.* New York: Alyson, 2006.

David Moats	*Civil Wars: A Battle for Gay Marriage.* Orlando, FL: Harcourt, 2004.
David G. Myers and Letha Dawson Scanzoni	*What God Has Joined Together? A Christian Case for Gay Marriage.* San Francisco, CA: HarperSanFrancisco, 2005.
William Naphy	*Born to Be Gay: A History of Homosexuality.* Port Stroud, UK: Tempus, 2006.
Dale O'Leary	*One Man, One Woman: A Catholic's Guide to Defending Marriage.* Manchester, NH: Sophia Institute Press, 2007.
Jonathan Rauch	*Gay Marriage: Why It Is Good for Gays, Good for Straights, and Good for America.* New York: Times Books, 2004.
Rich C. Savin-Williams	*The New Gay Teenager.* Cambridge, MA: Harvard University Press, 2005.
Leonard Sax	*Why Gender Matters: What Parents and Teachers Need to Know about the Emerging Science of Sex Differences.* New York: Doubleday, 2005.
Judith E. Snow	*How It Feels to Have a Gay or Lesbian Parent: A Book by Kids for Kids of All Ages.* New York: Harrington Park, 2004.
Darren Spedale	*Gay Marriage: For Better or For Worse? What We've Learned from the Evidence.* New York: Oxford University Press, 2006.

Peter Sprigg *Outrage: How Gay Activists and Liberal Judges Are Trashing Democracy to Redefine Marriage*. Washington, DC: Regnery, 2004.

Glenn T. Stanton and Bill Maier *Marriage on Trial: The Case Against Same-Sex Marriage and Parenting*. Downers Grove, IL: InterVarsity Press, 2004.

Laura Weibgen *U.S. National Debate Topic 2005–2006: U.S. Civil Liberties*. Bronx, NY: H.W. Wilson, 2005.

Glenn Wilson and Qazi Rahman *Born Gay: The Psychobiology of Sex Orientation*. London: Peter Owen, 2005.

Liz Winfield *Straight Talk about Gays in the Workplace*. New York: Harrington Park Press, 2005.

Evan Wolfson *Why Marriage Matters: America, Equality, and Gay People's Right to Marry*. New York: Simon and Schuster, 2004.

Index

I

J

K

L

M

N